LUCAS F.M

Beyond the Curtains:
Redefining Modern Relationships

ACKNOWLEDGEMENTS

I would like to express my deepest gratitude to the almighty God, for blessing me with the ideas, wisdom, inspiration and strength to write this book. His guidance has been my inspiration throughout this journey.

Table of Contents

PREFACE

Writing this book has been a journey of both reflection and discovery. The inspiration for this work came from my deep interest in the dynamics of modern relationships, a topic that continues to evolve in the face of changing social, cultural, and technological landscapes.

In a world where relationships are increasingly complex, I felt compelled to explore and share insights that could help individuals navigate these challenges with clarity and understanding. My goal is to provide not just advice, but to spark conversations that encourage people to think critically about their connections with others.

This book is a culmination of my thoughts, observations, and the wisdom I've gathered through personal experiences, as well as from those around me. While writing, I've come to appreciate how deeply relationships shape our lives and the ways in which we can cultivate healthier, more fulfilling connections.

I hope this book serves as a helpful guide to anyone seeking to understand the complexities of modern relationships, offering not just knowledge, but practical advice for creating lasting, meaningful bonds.

So, let's talk about it shall we, one of the most contended subjective issues in our societies right now, relationships. What is really going on? Where did it all start? And where is it headed towards?

We'll take a look at the difference in the matter between male and female, what is actually influencing both of their behaviors in weddings and relationships, what's up with feminism and how about masculinity, I can't believe there's something actually called "toxic masculinity and toxic feminist", what is it doing to the men and women, and the young boys and girls. Do people even still follow their hearts or minds or gut or whatever anymore, or are they just listening to the people who think they know everything about relationships on social media and gender communities, when in reality they're all just victims of heart breaks and relationship failures trying to spread their pain to others. The so called "dating experts and coaches" on the internet.

What's up with the now trending issue of the so called Alpha male, the Sigma male, the Beta male, Omega male and so on. And what about the so called Simps, both men and women simping!

And is marriage even still a thing today, or is it just the wedding that matters.

And talk about MGTOW "Men Going Their Own Way", I can't believe they even put it in initials.

Ok, clearly there's a lot to discuss here, so let's take a bite at it one at a time.

DISCLAIMER: Just remember that I'm not a relationship expert, coach or therapist. You can consider me an idealist or a theorist, which ever works, I just scour around looking on what is going on in our society, analyze it, look at the stats, apply my own theories and ideas, put it all into writing and "PRESTO!" you now have an idea of what's going on in your society. And you know what's the weird part? A lot of the things I observe mixed with my own theories and ideas usually tend to be considered as facts, with just a little bit of this and a little bit of that and you've got the right information.

Let's begin now shall we!

PERSPECTIVES

Quick overview just, when we talk about today's relationships, I have to say it, they're really messed up, it just doesn't feel like love anymore, so much dumping going around, the number of heartbreaks keeps going up, and I'm not even talking about the divorce rates these days. It just feels like there's no more love these days. I think it's time to play that song called "Where Is the Love?".

We've traded love and exchanged it for lust and money, literally, just look around, the number of women getting played by men keeps going up without getting married, its either getting left as a single mother or just a played and used single woman.

And just look at the men who are used for their money and resources, then getting dumped and start feeling like losers, there is a known fact that women live longer than men, why do you think that is? Well scientifically its proven, one of the causes is depression and what's one of the major causes of the depression, "heartbreaks", that's what it is, a guy can actually think that he's finally found the right girl, but in reality she's there just for the money and the free goodies, as soon as that's all gone, it's time for the girl to flee, leaving the guy heartbroken and depressed. Just be careful girls, because what may be an end result to this, the guy may consider the only solution to end all this is suicide, and we both know that isn't pretty for anyone.

Look around, the social media is filled with motivational speakers, either a man motivating his fellow men to stop wasting time on women and focus on their goals in life, talking about how relationships is for losers, saying that legends only are always single, and you know what? Most of those men are just the victims of heartbreaks who after getting played or dumped, their hearts turned black and decided to share their pain with others in an indirect way, by trying to warn them of avoiding girls and that girls are a waste of time. What's the end game for this? Guys who are single to old age without marrying, no one to look after them at old age, except for maybe retirement homes, no children, this is just depressing.

OR, we've got female feminists, as they are called that way in the social media trying to spread the message to their fellow women that women don't need men, saying that women are also capable of anything just as men are, some even go a step further saying that women should be on top and be dominant to men and women can do anything on their own. And what is the end result for this? Women get left lonely, unmarried, literally no man approaching them, regret of why they thought they could do it all on their own, and a lot of single mothers these days. It's all just sad.

But the sad reality of all these so called "motivational speakers", is that they all don't know what they're doing, they're literally not relationship coaches or experts, and in the end, they all end up in the same way, but by the time they realize it, it's too late, they're either single, divorced, single parents or just playing lonely.

Before we go even deeper let's take a look back at what relationships were like in the old years. Back then relationships were, should I say precise, it's either you love or you don't.

When we take a look at it in the men's perspective, back in the days, men's minds weren't mostly focused on women or using most of their time trying to find the perfect girl or just playing around with women, they knew in their mind that they needed a woman for one specific goal, reproduction, that is continuing their families, generation and legacies, as compared to modern men, these days a large percent of what's in the minds of men these days is actually women, literally someone can wake in the morning thinking about a girl, how to approach her which can even result to looking for help on the internet, and I mean it, there are hundreds of videos on the internet that teach men how to approach a girl, how to flirt with a girl, how to get a girl, and what to do if the girl rejects you or the plan backfires. There's literally a step for everything nowadays. Some men these days consider taking it slow in what they call basic step plan to get the girl of their dreams, become friends with her first, get to know her, make her laugh, a plan that could even take months. It's like taking a training course.

But what did the men in the old days do? Well that's easy, they see a girl, they approached the girl, went straight forward with it then, it was either a rejection or an approval. If it was approved, then it's a win, if it was a rejection, the man didn't just care because he knew there was an abundance of women to go around. And seeing that the most population of people in the world is actually females, you can see why and how they had this mindset. Men in the past knew that there were far greater things to achieve in life than to day dream the whole day away over women, they knew there was a world to build, a life to live, a legacy to carry on. They even at times just considered women as distractions, because they knew that they have to build their life first things' first and invite a woman later on. Because you know why they considered women as the last priority? As nature has set it, women are actually attracted to things that are more built up if I may say so, they're attracted to the men that look like they've got it all figured out. Don't get me wrong though, sometimes you may find the woman that is with you from your scratch to your highest achievements, and it's truly beautiful. But we'll touch on this point further on.

You see everything around you, everything built by man, all those efforts were put in at the cost of avoiding distractions like women. Let me ask you something. If men back then had the mindset of men today of constantly day dreaming of women, do you think we would be seeing all these achievements we are seeing now? You can answer that on your own.

Now let's shift on to the women's perspective, I got to tell you, back then there were no such things as boss ladies, feminism, or women empowerment, because women knew what they were supposed to do and be who they were supposed to be, a feminine woman. As I have said earlier, women are most likely to be attracted to the man who seems to have everything worked out for him. The guy who looks more masculine, the guy who has a higher status, the guy with a certain amount of wealth, this is what was most likely to attract a woman to a man. Because you know why? Some of the things women need from men is a guy that can provide, a guy that can protect, a guy that can lead. Women are beings for caring and nurturing, not providing and protecting. They're supposed to care and nurture for the man. Now let's compare them to the modern woman, the woman that says "what men can do, even women can do it", the one that emphasizes on equality, the one that shouts out feminism. Honestly, this is all stupid. You've got women these days saying that they're hustling to build their life, to provide for themselves, and I think we can both witness that most of these women a large percent of them usually end up unmarried or just single mothers, because they're messing with the balance of nature.

Women nowadays don't want to nurture and care for men, they want it to be 50/50 for each other, that is, everyone provides, everyone protects, everyone cares and everyone nurtures, something that is actually impossible. You can't mess with gender roles. Now let me ask you this, if women think that being 50/50 is the best thing, then why are large number of relationships and marriages crumbled and the so called boss ladies end up unhappily unmarried?

GENDER ROLES

Gender roles! What are the gender roles as assigned by nature to men and women?

As I have said it earlier, both male and female have their specific roles to play, whether be it a relationship or a marriage. Men are the protectors and providers. Women are the nurturers and care providers, which translates to men are supposed to get up, go out and fight for the necessities and bring back what they could get, protect his loved ones (which are basically family, girlfriend or wife, children) end of discussion. Likewise, as for women they're supposed to care for what the man has provided and brought back home and provide nurture to the man, that is make him feel at peace, make him feel comfortable, make him feel at home, give him what he needs (which is basically food, peace and sex), respect him as a man, and obey him because a man is the head, remember that. That's literally all it takes to build a healthy relationship or marriage.

But nowadays, people had to say, NO! there's so much more that can be done, why not switch it up a bit, why not assign men's roles to women, why not make it 50/50, why not give men jobs to women, the system is honestly messed up, and people don't even realize it.

Just take a look at what's happening around, divorce rates are higher than ever, a study was conducted and found out that in recent years 40%-50% of marriages end up in divorce and the number keeps rising. The number of diseases and illness resulting from mental issues is unspeakable. You can go around and see a man just sitting around completely out of it, what's he thinking about so much that got him stuck? Love is the answer, a woman. The number of men ending up in suicide because of heartbreaks keeps going up and up. Please bring back the good old days.

It has come a time where men have decided that it is pointless to marry anymore, literally have resulted to giving up on love and marriage, because they seem to have no purpose anymore, what is it if your woman tells you that she can also provide and protect, these are the things that fuel a man, these are what fill his purpose, but hearing it come from a woman just makes the man feel unimportant and decide that he should just protect and provide for himself.

And what's more surprising is that there are even some parents that are literally even telling their kids if they want to marry, then go ahead, if they don't want to, that's ok too, think about it, the parents, the ones who literally keep asking and questioning about when their son or daughter is eventually going to marry or get married, and sometimes even enforce their kids to do so, because they want grandchildren and see that time is flying by really fast. But now seeing how relationships are messed up nowadays, they're now down to saying "marry if you want or don't if you don't want to".

What people seem to misunderstand here is that nobody created these roles and assigned them to a particular gender, nobody said that men should do this, women should do this. These roles are all part of the balance of nature, it's a man's nature to provide and protect, it's a woman's nature to care and support. Why do you think things usually don't work out once a particular gender decides to play the part of the other gender? Because you're messing with the natural balance.

Look I'm no preacher here but just take a look at even the holy books, there are clearly roles assigned to each of the two genders, and once you narrow all the explanations down, you'll realize a woman's role is to care and listen to the man, and the man's job is to provide and protect for his loved ones. Now some assumptions have been regarded that because women think they're supposed to just stay and listen to their man, then they're not important. Who told you that?! Each and everyone's role is just as important as the other's.

One man put it best in simple words saying "Women are truly magnificent creatures. You give her a house, she'll give you a home, you give her ingredients, she'll give you a meal, you give her a sperm, she'll give you a child". Now from all of that, you tell me if you as a man or woman if a woman's job is not as important.

Now speaking for the man, what does he give? He has to be strong enough to protect his family, he has to be smart enough to guide his family, he has to be confident enough to take risks to provide for his family and has to be mature enough to know how to raise and lift his family. Everyone here has equally important roles to play.

Look around, who built this world, who took the risks of ensuring the world continues to develop and built all the great things that we see today, Men, and look around who multiplied this population on earth to give birth to the people that built this world, Women. But what's disappointing these days is that there are actually women communities (so called feminists) that are courageously saying that men are useless and are not needed in the society, who's going to build this world one day when you wake up and realize that all the men are gone? And there are some men out there saying the world would be a much better place if women hadn't existed, then who's going to multiply this world and fill it with more great people that will provide more great inventions and discoveries to grow this world?

Honestly speaking, I have to say shame on those people who say that they want it to be 50/50 in both a relationship and in marriages, you saying it to be 50/50 is like saying "if the woman gives birth, then so should the man, if the man can protect, then so should the woman" which is actually just messed up, everyone should stick to their natural balance roles, trust me, relationships where everyone knows what they're supposed to be and do are usually the ones that end up a lot happier than others, a relationship where the man knows he has to fight to provide for his wife and child and where the woman knows he has to love and be submissive to his husband, are the relationships that thrive because there is usually the working natural balance in order. There were literally studies conducted to see which relationships thrived and were the happiest the most, and the results were as said, the ones with the natural balance of order.

Anyways, I think by now you've got a slight clear understanding on how these gender role things work here and how they're clearly assigned to each gender. And though each gender has their own role to play towards society or towards their partners, the society still has different ways of treating or should I say teaching each gender how to be a man towards a woman and how to be a woman towards a man, and what the consequences are or what might be if they don't play their roles accordingly. We'll touch on that in the coming chapter.

SOCIETY VS GENDER EXPECTATIONS

You know, despite natures assignment of roles on each of the particular gender, both men and women, society still has large amounts of expectations on each of these two genders. And I don't mean to sound skeptical, but particularly men. Hear me out first. Just think about it, men are the only gender that are loved under certain conditions, different from women, but we'll touch on women's expectations from society also.

Let's start with the men. Men are expected to be the most gender that are supposed to be loved and cared for under the assumption that they should first provide something, that's right, you want a girlfriend, you have to show that you must provide something first, you want a wife you have to show that you have what is supposed to attract a wife, if you don't, then stand aside and let the men who can and has it all handle this. But what are these things that a man is expected to offer to get what he wants? Well that's easy money, status, skills, smarts, strength, the ability to provide, the ability to protect, the ability to win every time and the list goes on and on. Yeah, that's a heavy load when you think about it, why do you think men are the ones with the highest ranking of number of suicides in the society? Just think about it, a man has to have all these and probably even more just to get a girlfriend or a wife, why wouldn't someone suffer from constant rumination. Though don't get me wrong, it is a man's job to protect and provide just as I said earlier before, so there's really no way out of this, but this just goes to show you what a man has to be and has to go through to get what he wants. Just look at it, if a man wants to get respect from his partner, he has to show her his strong, he has to show her he's physically fit, he's smart, he's financially well (especially in these days), he can satisfy her, any man that can't achieve all this is left feeling left out, that's why the only motivation for a man to achieve success is everyone just telling him "hustle, there's no other way out. Life isn't easy for a man". This is literally the only advice a man is told to get back up on his feet and keep fighting to get what he wants, either the girl or respect, because there is no other way out.

You know what's weird, there's a story about a girl who had male features, not a transgender, but literal physical appearances, one day she decided to do a test where she would pose as a man and feel what it's like to be a man for a year, you know, the usual, talk to girls, work, and the rest of what men do and try to understand what men feel like in the society. You know what happened? She committed suicide at the end of the year! Shocking isn't it? She couldn't believe what men had to go through just to get some respect and love from society and girls. She couldn't bear the pain of seeing how men were disrespected by even their own wives just because they couldn't provide one thing, how society mistreated them just because they couldn't do one thing. That girl died knowing the reality of men's lives. Men understand this and they certainly understand there's no other way out but hustle and grind their way out. They know if they want a woman, then they have to earn their way to get her, because they know the only woman that can love them unconditionally is their mother. So it's the reality for men, and you know what? Nobody cares what men have to go through, all they want to see is what they've got. What's that quote? "Nobody cares about your hustles or how you got there, all they want to see are the results". And that's how it is for men, that's the cold hard truth.

So, for my fellow men out there, just keep hustling, there's no other way out.

Now let's move on to the women's side. Now what does the society and men expect from women? Well honestly speaking, it's more of the attractive aspect, which is basically, beautiful, sexy and also caring, these are literally what women need to have as expectations from society. Why do I say beautiful and sexy? Because that's what society looks at the most, a woman who is beautiful and sexy gets twice the attention from people as compared to normal looking women, men and even women notice a woman who's beautiful and attractive, whether she's pretty, or has a curvaceous shape. Look, it's no secret that any attractive woman that walks by or down the street will get heads to turn and look her way, because she's beautiful and even sexy, and because men and society know very well that she's got it all, then it's easy for men to approach her making her have a huge number of options in men to choose from, and even easier for her to get hired at different places like modelling, acting and wherever else, seriously, if a normal girl and a very attractive and sexy girl both go looking for a job, who do you think will easily get the position? Easily it's the attractive one, even though professionally she may not be the one fit for the position. And why do I say caring? Well that's the biggest thing a proper man looks for in a woman to make her his partner, just as I said earlier care and support. Honestly beauty and sexy attract the man but what's guarantee to keep him is the care, we'll touch on that later on. So, you can see here even women are expected to have certain traits and qualities, and they know this, that's why the number of women makeup, fashion divas and plastic surgery keeps going up. The truth is that it hurts some women to do this stuff and keep up with it but they know there is no other option, some women aren't the makeup kind or body enhancement type, but because they think and know that society and men have expectations, of which some may seem a bit unreal, they don't have much of an option.

So it's either you're beautiful, sexy and caring to get men and societal approval, but if you're not then what's the fate? Alone, single, unapproachable and left out. But this is what the society has decided, everyone must play a particular role and have particular expectations reached, it may seem unfair, but even if you shout it out, I don't think it'll change anything, so the best option is adapt and survive. But sometimes these expectations may sound a bit unfair, just look at it, this means that only the most beautiful and sexy women are approached by men and seduced by rich dudes, and the fate of the women that fail to meet these expectations leaves them feeling emotionally hurt and even physically damaged, literally, the number prostitutes or sex workers keeps rising, why? Some may know and others may not, it's because some of these girls feel like they're not enough to keep up with societal expectations, can't make a living because they're not pretty enough, and no man approaches them, so as a way of not feeling left out they result to this, and what else? Go through painful body enhancement surgeries just to get the attention of men, of which some of these enhancements don't usually end up the way they're supposed to, resulting in critical impairment and sometimes even results to painful death, so it's pretty rough when you look at it.

Look, there's really no way to change society's expectations, it's like they were there since the dawn of civilization, like I said, you either adapt and survive, or don't and accept the hard fate. It's like a set of rules that are already signed and approved for, men have to be strong, smart and resourceful to attract the woman and get society's respect, women have to be beautiful and caring to get the man and fit in.

You know this reminds me mostly of the animal kingdom, we're literally living just like they are, the male animal has to be the strongest, the most courageous, the most resilient and the most resourceful to attract the mate and earn respect. And the woman, has to be the most attractive to grasp the male's attention at all time. And what of the animal that has lost this race? Easy, it's the end for it, unless it comes back better than before. Yeah, the resemblance is uncanny.

Anyway, the hard truth is that these expectations are already in place and they may also be a factor in some relationships. I mean just look at it, it has reached to a point that men have to fake it to get it, men have to fake it to get the woman, and social media has helped with that, nowadays men can literally just post some flashy car and big building, dress in high status fashions just to get the women's approval, and you know what? It actually works, because the woman will think this guy's made it, he can provide for me and cater to my needs, but what happens when the truth is found out that he has nothing, then comes the disrespect, the disapproval and disavow. And another cold hard truth is that the expectations women have on men have also become somewhat unrealistic that some men have even decided to give up on dating, relationships and even marriage, because apart from the expectations, most women have shown that they're not ready to settle for the ordinary guy who seems like he doesn't have it all figured out just yet, but rather have shown that they want the guy who's already complete, the full package and rather not hear the guy who says he's working hard on getting what she or they need. That's why you see so many women nowadays aren't getting married, the problem is high or even unrealistic expectations.

But what about the women? Honestly speaking, they've learnt that good looks are what grabs a man's attention and good looks are what brings a lot of men their way, so what to do now? Put on a ton of make up till you come out looking like a something from a horror movie. What else? Change the physical appearance, why not enlarge the breasts and the butt size to the point you look like a real life made up action figure toy. Because they know it's what grasps men's attention, you've heard of the saying "men love what they see and women love what they hear, that's why women wear makeup and men lie", this is how it applies here.

But you know what's the saddest part of all this is? The women that get the man who have everything resource-wise still end up feeling unsatisfied, why? Because deep down they will soon come to realize that under all that money and expensive things, there is no true love, genuine love can never be bought. And what about the men that get the women that have the beauty and the looks? Well they soon come to realize that good looks and beauty don't really compensate for building a well standing relationship. And you know, the harsh reality here is that these women most of the time don't really get married, and all this is because of the misinterpretation that good looks attract a man, sure they attract a man, but they don't necessarily keep the man. So basically it's a loss for both.

This is what high number of expectations from society and both genders have led to, making people feel like they're just not enough anymore and thus needing to go the extra mile just to get the approval everyone thinks is necessary to get. But hey, at least now you know right.

STANDARDS

Now let's take a look at something else that's a bit on the heavy side, standards. Let's be honest here, everyone at some point in life sets their own set of standards they want to get in life, but there comes a time that these standards just seem a bit over the top and start to seem as if it would be better for someone with high account of standards to create their own world and their own kind of people.

Preferably, in modern relationships, there seems to be a high number of standards set by a gender. Particularly in today's world, it seems that women have set the standards bar so high that men have decided that it is impossible to satisfy modern women and left them hanging with their seemingly impossible standards. Another reason why the marriage rates these days are so low. But that doesn't mean that men don't have their own standards, surprisingly it has reached to a point that men's standards are even said to be demonized, what does this mean you may wonder? It means that men's standards are seen as wicked, because we now live in an era where when a man has certain standards about a kind of woman he wants, he's seen as being selfish, arrogant, and even a misogynistic, but when a woman has her standards, there's no problem. Why? Because this is a time in life where women are now being empowered, where women now have a voice of speaking and being heard whatever they want to say and do, where women who think they can live independent of men, where women think a man needs to be the complete package just to get a girl, and despite the challenges that a man has to go through to get these achievements, society and women don't care, as I said before, your results are all that matter, not what you're struggling with or what you went through. Now because of this, men have realized that sometimes it can be impossible to satisfy both societal and women expectations, thus the best thing to do is just stay single and build by themselves for themselves.

To make a proper explanation of what both men and women's standards are like, let's drop them down shall we;

Let's start with men's standards. What standards does a man want in a woman?

- ❖ Respect: This is the number one standard that men want in a woman, and it is the biggest standard above all, have you ever heard that a man would rather be respected than loved? Now you have. All a man wants in his entire life is respect, that's why a man would never go the extra mile to ruin his own respect, if it reaches a point where a man realizes that the woman his with doesn't respect him anymore or rarely shows him even an inch of respect, just know it won't be long for him to end it. And come on, this is reasonable, every human wants respect.

- ❖ Appreciation: The second standard is appreciation, it feels nice every once in a while to feel appreciated, who doesn't like to be appreciated? I do. And it feels extra nice to be appreciated by your lover.

- ❖ Submissive: Nothing screams sexy to a man than a woman who is submissive, a man knows a woman can be really beautiful, but if she's not submissive, it's nothing to him.

- ❖ Caring: A caring woman is what keeps a good man, a man knows the caring isn't just for him, but he knows that a caring woman is able to well handle his family.

- ❖ Neat: What aspects of neatness am I talking about here? Well for starters there's clean, smart, well attractive, she doesn't have to be the most rose in the cactus pile, but able to maintain her appearance.

Honestly speaking, that's pretty much what a man's standards are on the woman he wants to have, but in today's society there is the so called demonizing of men's standards and we call them too selfish and rather consider women's standards to be more reasonable. So what are the women's standards? Let's take a look shall we;

- ❖ Smart: The obvious, no woman wants a man that's anything but smart, you know how it goes, you've got to look to impress.

- ❖ Attractive: The classic, women desire a man that's attractive and appealing to the eyes, the handsome man with particular facial features.

- ❖ Financially stable: I don't mean to say every woman on the planet, but it's well known that women want a man that can financially provide in the house to keep her in the house.

- ❖ Desired by other women: This is a weird one though, apparently modern women mostly desire the man that is mostly desired by other women, because they believe if they all want him, then he's got to have something special to give.
- ❖ Pays for everything: In addition to paying for need stability, women also desire a man that is able to pay for apparently everything, from his own bills to her bills as well, and everything else apparently.
- ❖ Protective: A woman wants a man who can protect and feel safe at all time.
- ❖ Confident: One of the things observed to turn on women is a man's confidence, if a man lacks confidence apparently they don't see him as a complete man.
- ❖ A good listener: As it is well known, women are usually talkative. No lie there, which means they want a man who can listen to her at all time.
- ❖ Good in bed: That's right, you heard it, women desire a man who can satisfy them in bed, man who can make them fill pleasured at all time.
- ❖ Comforter: In addition to that, women want a man who can comfort them, the charmer, Mr. Romantic, the guy who can make them feel good about themselves.
- ❖ Dominant man: Despite being a comforter, women also want the man who appears to be dominant, the man who can put her in her place when she messes up.
- ❖ Mature: Women want a man who is mature enough to tell them what to do, something like a leader persona.
- ❖ Gives her attention: Women are the creatures well known to be attention seekers, so another standard that women have is that the man must give her his attention almost all the time, compliment her and make her feel good about herself.

Ok I think that's enough, clearly you can see for yourselves here that some standards might seem a bit too much and sometime even maybe impossible to achieve all these. But does matter it what the man thinks? Absolutely not! Because you either got it or you don't. Women today have completely and utterly digested the notion that they're entitled to a certain kind of lifestyle that's supposed to be offered by the man, they claim to want a man who's rich, successful, famous, well-built physically, smart, a man who'll spoil her, spend expensive and unnecessary things on her, take her to expensive vacations a lot and more.

Because of all these it's why men these days are refusing to marry, because most of them know that no one man can meet all these standards. And because women see that men cannot have all these traits, they've decided to turn the table and decided that women can be independent and handle themselves. But you know what, the truth is that no one man can handle all these standards because no one is complete, unless you create your own human. That's why women these days who are in a relationship have something called "The backup plan". This "backup plan" is well explained in a theory made by the famous King Arthur long ago, he called it the "The Round Table Theory". The theory depicting just how, especially in modern relationships, one partner is simply not enough to satisfy someone.

If you don't know what "The Round Table Theory" is, then listen up.

ROUND TABLE THEORY

The round table theory simply meant that no one man can easily satisfy one woman. Each man sitting around the table is supposed to bring something meaningful and helpful to the table to be seen as valuable, if you don't have anything to give, then simply you are not seen as valuable. Picture this, a table with a whole fried chicken on it, one man comes with the sauce, another man comes with the spices, another comes with the utensils, and each man must come with something to be allowed to eat the chicken, if you don't have anything, then just don't seat at the table and no eating for you. Now in place of the chicken put a woman, and every man has to come up with something that's beneficial to the woman to allow him to get with her. What is that something? Well that's easy, money, good looks, fame, pleasure and every other woman's fantasies of a man of her dreams. Things are starting to clear up aren't they? This is what the round table theory discussed, that no one man can satisfy a woman, instead a woman has several men for several purposes and several occasions.

Since women know that their man can't provide all their needs and wants at once, they've resulted to applying this theory in real life, I think you can see this too, one woman exploiting up to 7 men for her own pleasure, and I heard there are even women going as far as up to 60 men, that's too much even for one girl, seriously. Anyways, one woman several boyfriends, and each one has a vital role to play in the woman's life. There is a man who pays the bills, all the woman's bills are covered by this guy, the electricity bill, rent, taxes, credit card bills, medical bills, phone bills and any other bill you can think of. There is the one for sex, this is the guy who's having the real pleasure of the woman, the one to fulfill the woman's bed desires, this guy mostly doesn't have to pay for anything, mostly these are the ones termed as the bad boys, toxic guys, the guys who don't give a shit, they're the ones that turn the women on, all he does is just satisfy her and that's it, and what's even weirder is that the men who pay for the woman's expenses sometimes never even get to lay with her in bed, she'll just have them as standby ATM machines. Then there's the one for cuddling purposes, this is Mr. charming, the one who knows how to make the woman feel good about herself, whenever she's in a bad mood, shell know who to call to cheer her up and make her head filled with pride again. Then comes the guy for shopping, handbags, new cloths, new shoes, new hair, anything, you name it and this guy's got it. The one for finding her a job, there is actually a man who's there just to help the woman find a job, whether it's after her college or just searching for a job. Then there's the guy that every girl wants, this guy might have masculine features or fame that attracts other women, now in women's fantasies, if a guy attracts other women, she'll also want him, just because he's wanted by other women, whatever it is that attracts them doesn't really matter, as long as they want him, she'll want him too. Then finally there's the boyfriend, the guy known to have gone and seduced her and she said "yes", the one who even her friends know him as the boyfriend, sad isn't it?

Anyways, back to the theory, it clearly shows that each man for the woman plays his own part, and once the man's role is over, then there's no need for him to sit at the table anymore. What this means is that once the bill paying guy runs out of money, it's a breakup, once the shopping guy can't afford it anymore, it's bye-bye, once the cuddling guy can't make her feel special anymore, then don't waste her time anymore, and even when the boyfriend isn't a good impression anymore, it's an easy "we should see other people" text from her. And until she can find another man who's better in bed, the sex guy might still stick around for the meantime.

This is how relationships are nowadays, frustrating, disgusting, and depressing in a nutshell.

Speaking of back up plans, it has even come to a time when men have their own back up plans, though it's a bit different from women, there isn't a girl for electric bills, or shopping or whatever, instead men have a backup plan in case the girl they're with seems difficult to handle or has suddenly become arrogant or proven to be different than when she was at first, mostly in relationships men need sex, peace of mind, respect and care, that's why I said this is a bit different from women. Ever heard of the statement "Men stay where there's peace"? Well, to men, those things are their peace, if the girl she's with starts to bring out weird drama and negative attitudes, he won't settle for it, he'll just go to the backup plan and get peace, or if where he is he's not getting sex from his girl, not a problem, he'll just go to the backup girl and get it, that's why in terms of cheating mostly men and women differ. Women cheat in regarding their emotions, men cheat regarding mostly physical aspects.

Well now that you know what the round table theory is and how it works, think about that the next time you see your girl having something that you couldn't afford for her or went somewhere she wanted to go but you couldn't take her, because remember, 'when your dog starts barking at you then there might be someone else feeding it better'.

 Or realize that when your man comes back happy and calm suddenly after you caused him unnecessary drama or gave him negatives vibes or starts looking like he's pulling away from you without explanation.

Now that that's covered, let's move on and start looking at the movements that are widely spreading in the societies and have an impact on the relationships nowadays.

FEMINIST MOVEMENT (FEMINISM)

Now let's take a look at one of the movements that inspired equality among the two genders of both men and women, the women movement or sometimes referred to as a community, the movement that said whatever men can do, women can also do it. It started out as something that specifically aimed at to give women their own rights, a harmless little community to make sure women aren't treated with disrespect or oppressed in any way, but today it has sparked quite the dilemma in modern times, especially in marriages and relationships, bringing the whole idea of 50/50, perverting the minds of young girls and women that women and men should be seen as equal and if a man can stand alone, then a woman can and should stand alone also, if a man is on top, then a woman should be on top also. It is quite frantic actually.

A little background first. Feminism has its roots dating back centuries ago and began to gain momentum in the late 19th century and early 20th centuries, as I said it started out as a harmless community aiming to ensure women were advocated for their rights during the societal shifts such as the industrialization and urbanization period, which then provided opportunities for women to engage in public life and advocate for their rights, again 'harmless'. But as years kept on going and as the community grew and grew and social media kept growing and spreading, new ideas of the community started evolving started giving the thought to women that "hey, why should men be the only ones to lead, why should men be the only ones to be at the top, why should men be the only ones that can become successful and independent?". Those ideas are today the major causes of relationship failures, highly increasing rate of divorces, women remaining single mothers, men refusing to marry, increasing rate of successful women that are single and lonely who result to being "sugar mummies"! Clearly this harmless little movement has evolved and a lot of problems has evolved a lot with it.

You know, having something to help advocate for your rights and make sure you're not oppressed in any way is not a bad thing, but going to the extent of declaring that everything should be 50/50 and women should be allowed to lead, that's something completely different. Don't take this personal girls, but the truth is that women can't lead, and it's not because of some problems with women, no, it's because it's their nature, women weren't meant to lead, as I said before, women are to care and nurture, you can't just take a man's role and stick it on you and expect it to work, it doesn't work like that, each gender has their own role to play in the ecosystem.

And honestly speaking, when it comes to the concept of 50/50, that's not a real thing, there are actual women that want what men are offered, the same job, the same respect, the same positions, the same roles, "what a man can do, a woman can do it too" this is what roams around the modern women's heads right now. And it's even going as far as some women want men to take on the women duties and roles, sooner or later they're going to want men to also get pregnant. Just my thoughts on this, because really the situation is bad now.

But that's not all, feminism has gone to the point that women can be independent and successful without the help of men, there's a literal term for this, "Boss lady", "the queen of her own empire", "single lady standing alone", you can literally see girls nowadays posting on social media how she just bought a new house, or that new luxury car, or that designer brand, while putting quotes like "Instead of crying after a boy, live like a queen", or "hot girl summer time". And they all look happy achieving all that, but are they really? Well on photos that's obviously a yes, to the extent that other girls get jealous that they also want a life like that, a strong independent woman living life on her own terms. But just remember this, those same girls are the ones who later on start seeking for any man to be with, literally anyone, just as long as they have someone by their side, if you've also noticed is that how come most of the so called strong independent women are usually the ones who later on marry just some regular guy or sometimes even a bum, or are the ones that advertise themselves on the media that they're looking for a man to marry them, anyone as long as they'll love them, but these are the same women that said they wanted only their career and nothing else, why? Loneliness is the answer, you can put that career stuff ahead, that's fine and call yourself an independent whatever it is you want, but as the years go by, you'll soon start to realize that the only thing that mattered the most was building a happy and stable family and having someone beside you to love and care, but the saddest thing is that most of these women usually figure this out when years have gone by and everything and everyone around them has changed.

Look, don't get me wrong, there's nothing wrong with wanting to settle down and build a good life for yourself and your loved ones, but if this takes up too much of a priority in your life that nothing else matters, that you a woman don't need any man to be you, then you'll get the life you want, but in reality it won't be the life you need.

The other thing that feminism has ruined is going to the extent of somehow influencing women that men are not needed in the society. It's actually unbelievable that there are women who actually say that men are useless and are not needed, their argument is that men have no importance and women can do anything that men can do or did and men are just useless, just sad. But if you take a look, these are the same women who later on end up being miserable and lonely, these are the ones who usually end up saying "what's wrong with me, why can't I find a good man to settle down with", I don't know if that's karma or just nature taking its course. But usually the end is not really exciting.

This whole feminist thing started out with a good intention at first, just to make sure that women were considered in some aspects of life, make sure that women weren't bullied at some point, make sure that women were recognized that they too can be of help to the society, and that was fine, but nowadays it's just actually ruining the lives of younger women and even some men. How? Well if you take a look, you can see that feminism has made men seem inferior to women now, in relationships, in marriages (we'll touch on more of this on later chapters), there are relationships or marriages where the men are the ones getting bullied by their woman, this is because feminism has implanted in the minds of women that a woman can also be at the top like a man, its taught them that a woman doesn't have to be submissive to her man or husband, and upon absorbing this, the women do just that, try to overpower the man and make the man feel inferior, this can honestly cause a lot of tension to the men as they start to question themselves if women are actually worth dating or marrying anymore.

To understand just how feminism has ruined a lot of relationships or marriages nowadays, let me give you some examples or let's say confessions. There are women who actually have admitted that being a feminist for couple of years have brought them nothing but sorrow in the end, because they spent most of their years believing that they don't need a man in their life, men are of no good to them, blowing up any man that tries to come up to them, and in the end they got more than what they bargained for, as the years went by they started to realize they need a man in their life to love and care for them, they need a family, children, all that stuff, but because of the path they chose before, getting all this stuff now is near to almost impossible, because nature gives you what you give out, now no man wants to approach them, no matter where they go or what they try, it's almost as if they've become invisible to men, and that's where all the "WHY" questions start to pop up, "why don't men recognize me? Why doesn't any man come up to me? Why can't I find a good man to settle down with? Why can't I get married?" And in the end, they finally come up to confess that they've ruined their lives by trying to be a feminist, they have all the money, but end up crying realizing that it's not what they actually needed. That's the harsh reality. And apart from that, even most of the single mothers that supported feminism, came out crying and confessing that they really needed a partner to be with and help out with the parenting stuff, but because they set their minds out on being a strong independent woman, they regret everything they ever did or said, because once you've already said something or done something, you can't take it back, and every man will know that you're someone to stay away from.

And you know, a large influence of this feminism stuff comes from the social media world, this is what is brainwashing the modern girls and women and making them have these weird thoughts that they can and need to be a feminist, just think about it, where do most of the modern women spend their time on? And where are all the great examples of women advertising themselves as feminists? Each and every day you'll see women posting themselves as buying a new nice car, or buying a big house or expensive gifts and quoting themselves as "Queen of her own empire" or "Making money bitch" or "Chase the bag, don't chase the dude", and everyone else just replying "Get the dough girl" or "Slay queen, slay" or whatever, and these girls that usually reply to this are the ones who's minds get filled up with the junk that if the girls on these posts did it on their own without needing anyone and anything, then I can too, sure it can be a bit of a motivation, but the way that these posts are portrayed and the messages they convey is that women should stop wasting their time on men and build their life up, that's all they need, when in reality behind these posts not everything is as it appears to be, sure it's nice and all seeing their fellow girl get all the things that they could only dream of, but is that what really makes them happy in the end? Because sooner or later you'll come to realize that you may have gotten everything you've wanted, but it's not what you needed to truly make you happy and fulfilled as a woman. And later on as these women start to confess and testify their true feelings, it's really depressing how they end up like, satisfied but not fulfilled.

Because you need to realize there are two different things, you can be satisfied with all the things you wanted, but you can never fill fulfilled as long as you don't have the right things you need. I've seen women being with someone who only strives on one meal a day but their happiness is immeasurable and single women with enough money in their life to travel everyday yet are still miserable, Why? Because there's a difference between living in satisfaction and living in fulfillment.

This is what feminism is doing to people nowadays, particularly the women, but they usually don't see the effects of supporting this movement or being in such a community until it's too late. And that's how life hits you hard, you may think something is right just because everyone else is doing it, but the effects of what you've done or chosen can never be hidden, sooner or later reality will begin to unfold itself and show you the consequences of your actions or decisions.

Now, I guess that's all cleared up, let's get on to the masculine side of the movement, or masculinity or toxic masculinity as they've termed it.

MASCULINITY/TOXIC MASCULINITY

As we first saw feminism earlier, we learned of its aim to advocate for women's rights and give them equal opportunities to be recognized in the societies. Well masculinity is a bit like feminism, though it's for the opposite gender, men that is, and mostly it's just concerned with advocating for men's standards and their priorities, sometimes it's also a reminder to men what it means to be a man in today's societies.

Regardless of what it is or what its intentions are, it's considered as toxic, why is it toxic? Well that's easy, it's because men's standards are so called demonized or men who have certain standards are said to be misogynistic. The reality is that men are treated harshly in today's society, well in overall society if I may say so. Women are more considered and listened and even valued to than men in today's society, women are more favored than men. As I explained before, men are only loved or respected under the condition that they can provide something or have something valuable, fame, status, wealth, whatever, but without that you're just a passerby. And this is all about values, but we'll touch on that later on.

Speaking about masculinity on a more understandable term, it can simply mean men's priorities, it's what speaks for the men, just like how feminism speaks for the women. Let me give you an example, when a man says "I want a submissive, slim, young virgin girl", this is masculinity, these are his terms, they are his priorities, but as I said, upon saying or wanting things like these, he is considered as misogynistic and rated as toxic, hence the term toxic masculinity. Masculinity is the man's boundary to remind him that he is born a man, a human who from birth has no value on this planet, he should have certain expectations in his life, he should set certain principles in his life, he should have priorities and set boundaries for himself as a man, like having only friends that encourage him to grow, think about his future, because a man's fate is in his own hands, choose the perfect life partner to build a family with, choose a suitable career and build himself up from the bottom to shine his value.

Everything starting from physique, character, attitude, perceptions, principles all this is based on man's masculinity traits. When we compare feminism to masculinity, we can see that both may seem to have a particular aim for both genders to identify their rights, help them make proper decisions best for their future and make them aware of their values and what to do to boost their values and what not to do so as to avoid lowering or losing their values.

Now, there's this concept about demonizing masculinity or men's principles and standards as applied to masculinity traits. Like I said before, men's principles and standards are considered as toxic, therefore are termed to be demonized, a clear meaning of the word demonized is someone or something that is considered as evil or even worthy of contempt or blame. So by this explanation, it means that masculinity is considered as something that is evil, so when a man says he wants "a good job with a loyal submissive partner whose white, slim and not too demanding", he's considered as evil, but when a woman says she wants "a rich, six foot, handsome, famous guy who will take care of all her needs and provide everything she wants", it's understandable? This goes to show you just how men's standards are underrated and disapproved.

Though everything does have its bad side, despite masculinity being men's statement for what a man should be and how he should live and behave, sometimes it can take things a bit too far. For say it can be too harsh on women, we know women are supposed to be helped and protected, but masculinity may push the inferiority and superiority button a bit too much and consider women as weak and meant to be controlled like objects and puppets. This is probably one of the reasons that feminism rose up, to break the chains of oppression and being bullied by men, there's a difference between being led and being controlled and over dominated, sure a man can lead his woman, but not becoming too aggressive to the point that she starts fearing him instead, a woman can support her man in any ways, but don't let masculinity consider your woman as worthless and neglect her completely like some unimportant object.

Everything when pushed too far always has a bad side to it, sometimes masculinity imprints the idea of a lone wolf, it's understandable that sometimes doing things on your own is ok to blur out distractions and unnecessary hindrances, but masculinity can take the concept of lone wolf a bit too far to the extent that a man claims he doesn't need any help from anyone, he can do everything all on his own, look, despite you being a man and all of that, we are still humans, and no matter what principles or standards or rules we may set for ourselves, there still will be a time when we need help from others, it's human nature, there are somethings that require normal human nature, not even masculine traits can help you, but because of the law of masculinity that men should be independent, sometimes it makes it hard for a man to seek help from anyone else, whether it's medical or just emotional support.

Can I ask you something? What would you as a man expect in life? A good job or business, a good partner, a well thought out good future for you, your family and your kids, a secured financial freedom right? Well this is mostly expressed in the masculinity theme, typically it's a way to express men's requirement and desires in his life, take it as a code of conduct. If it's that good, then why is it demonized or considered as toxic then? It's just a way for men to express themselves of what they need, want and desire in life, to be fair it seems like men aren't actually having it easy in life, well that is the harsh truth actually, your desires or expectations don't actually matter to the society, you want a nice woman? Search for her, you want a nice car? Work for it, you want to secure financial independency? Work like a slave. This is the stone cold fact for the lives of men, nobody really gives a shit about what you want in life, all they see is the results, that's why as long as you're a man, you don't really have any other option but to get up and go get what you want, nobody's bringing it to you like a king, you have to work to make yourself the king.

Here's a good question, Let's say a man who's already made it in life, has all the money any man could ever dream of and he says "I want a beautiful, white, curvy, submissive, loyal girl", do you think people will call this man a misogynist or term him as toxic? Well easily no, sure maybe sometimes by modern women who know they won't fit the list, but in a high ratio, no, because he has everything well thought out for him, he has what people see, the results, so he is liable to get what he wants. But for the majority of us men who are still finding it hard and trying to make a living in life, whatever is it you say you want or desire in life, your answer will always be "good luck with that", but as soon as you have what society wants, you can say or have whatever it is you want, heck society will even help you choose it for you, that's why you'll hear certain people talk about a successful man like "that's the girl he's dating, he could've done better, he could've dated or married someone more better. That's the house he's living in, I thought he'd have a mansion living somewhere more exotic". All these just because the guy has the so called survival tools in life.

So, in short we can say that masculinity isn't considered toxic as long as you're successful. Well there you have it, so to the society and women, masculinity is considered toxic and that's why people that look like they're supporting masculinity are being demonized and termed as misogynistic, but as long as they have what everyone else wants, the money, the fame, the status, the power, they can get away with wanting or saying anything, all the more reason for men to struggle to build themselves up to have their way with what they want and desire, literally no other options here, survive or perish.

My views on this is, masculinity isn't all the way a bad thing, like I said, it's like a code of conduct for men, remind them of what it is to be a man, especially in today's society, and make them realize that men have it hard in the world until they've proven they can be valuable and offer some value. It is a nice movement, though the important thing to remember is regardless of any movement or community people can start, everything taken too far is bad, you know how the saying goes "too much of anything is harmful", we've seen just how both of these movements (feminism and masculinity) had proper intentions, but when digested too much is actually too dangerous for oneself and even to others.

Now that we've cleared those two out of the way, there's just one more community, that's not very popular, though has taken a quick and slow uprising that, is in both ways affecting both men and women, we need to see, and this in regards to feminism and masculinity is the craziest I've seen. It is a men's movement, that's not only changed the perception on how men view women, but also caused women to uphold the belief that men are no longer available, let's go see how men have decided to go their own way.

MGTOW (MEN GOING THEIR OWN WAY)

Like the name of the movement speaks for itself, Men Going Their Own Way. A brief explanation first of this movement. MGTOW first emerged in the early 2000's (the so called millennial years) where it primarily gained traction on online forums and communities and as the days and years went on, it has since spread to various offline communities, including meetups and podcasts.

So what was or is still the purpose of this movement? What is it doing? Well, typically it's a men's movement who believe in prioritizing their own well-being and independence often as a response to what they perceive as societal pressures and expectations placed on men or heavy burdens on men. It includes skepticism towards long-term relationships and marriage, as well as advocating for men's rights and autonomy.

But what was the main influence of this movement? Why did whoever start it initiate it in the first place? That's easy, the main influences of this movement was disillusionment with traditional gender roles, divorce laws, family court biases, and societal expectations placed on men. No wonder. Just picture it this way, as a man you're tired of society, family and friends expecting too much from you, you're tired of false and fake women and relationships, what do you do about it? Just start a movement to advocate for your wellbeing and independence. The philosophy of the movement encourages men to prioritize their own personal fulfillment and wellbeing over societal expectations or traditional paths like marriage and long-term relationships, some individuals in this movement even advocate for minimal involvement or avoidance of women altogether, while others focus on self-improvement, independence and pursuing their own goals and interests. So it's like an anti-women movement, as sometimes it is referred to as a misogynistic movement.

The context of MGTOW aims to influence men to first avoid women, second focus on their goals and interests and third, to develop independence of dropping expectations from society. in the context of relationships, it means men should avoid women altogether, as we have seen before, this may be as a result of women's standards, the rise of feminism and demonizing men, remember feminism began way even before this MGTOW stuff, so basically, men are so fed up of these false standards and rising women feminists power that they've decided to make their own movement, well it was bound to happen sooner or later. I mean seriously, just look around as society keeps expecting more from men, women keep bringing weird accusations on men in relationships terms, I think the question would've been why isn't there a men's movement to advocate men to stay away from women, so there you have it.

It's not exactly as popular as the other movements, but you know, everything starts out small. It's main roots as I said started out online, it was an online community influencing and educating men to stay away from relationships, marriages and women and just focus on their goals and interests, don't get me wrong, there may be a good side to this, sure it's fine that men are being influenced to just focus on their goals, but what about the other side, the fact that men should not focus on women at all and completely ignore them. The truth about this statement in reality is that it means there are no good women at all, every woman is bad that's why are told to completely forget about women, now that's the downside of it. One thing you should know is that this community, this MGTOW (Men Going Their Own Way) was typically initiated by men who went through a rollercoaster of hard and brutal relationships with women, so in the end had concluded that all women are evil and men should stay away from all women. So it's basically the result of some men's hurting. I'm not going to lie, it's true that some women make it hard for a man to believe if women are even worth seducing or coming up to talk to anymore, but that doesn't mean that every single woman on earth is completely like that, speaking from experience I know this and I've lived it.

You've probably seen or heard women nowadays saying that men no longer want to involve themselves with women at all, even the rates of marriages are dropping drastically. There are women even on social media who say that men are afraid of marriage responsibilities nowadays that's why they don't even partake in marriage or approaching girls anymore, well that's not true, one of the hard truth lies in this concept of men deciding to go their own way, who said men don't want to involve in marriage? Men are actually thrilled to start a family and continue their legacies through bloodlines, but on the account of what's happening nowadays with the whole women standards and societal expectations and men demonized thing, it's reached a conclusion that most men don't want women anymore and just focus on building themselves.

There are literally tons of books written by people on how MGTOW is a very good thing, and guess what they're primary emphasis is on? Avoiding women, liberation of men from the opposite gender, instructing single men on how to live by navigating away from the female gender, some books are written as instruction manuals on how to become a MGTOW and live the MGTOW way. Like I said before, this concept of MGTOW is merely a concept that was started by men who've been through heartache relationships, so it's like a way of them expressing their feelings, fine it's good to inspire fellow men to remember that they have goals to focus on and build their power, but really it just seems like an antifeminism movement, like how women have the feminist theme, now men have their own theme that goes against women, the antIfeminist community, and just like how feminism reminds and teaches women that women should be in power and men are useless, this is how MGTOW now teaches and reminds men that women are of no worth it, so it's basically a gender based community war, you can see how people have seriously lost it.

But seriously, the rise of all this MGTOW stuff is basically influenced from men who have been betrayed, used, hurt and been made a joke of in their past relationships. And honestly by the way relationships are working nowadays I'm not surprised they turned out this way, and what they're saying is mostly noticeable in a large number in our societies right now. What do I mean by this? Just look around, there's a category of men known as the nice guys or in another newer term "The Simps", we'll see more about this term in the next chapter though. The nice guys are usually the ones who are known as the ones who know how to handle or treat a woman right, they're the men that will go to great lengths to care for a woman, to make her happy, to save a woman, continuously gifting the woman, in short do anything necessary to make her comfortable and happy as they know or assume that this is the way to keep a woman and make her continue falling in love with the guy. If this is true and it's the way of making a woman stay, then why do they always run or go back to the so called bad boy or the naughty guy and ditch or betray the nice guy if he's giving her everything she wants? Women nowadays, if you've seen this habit around nowadays, would rather go back to the abusive, naughty, bad boy who won't give her the time of day, or who won't surprise her with shit, and it doesn't even matter if he's broke, still they'll choose him over the nice guy who may be even a multimillionaire. The nice guys are the ones betrayed, played, used and drained, over and over again, at last, what happens to someone who gets constantly betrayed over and over again? That's easy, their hearts become hardened, their emotions change, their attitude changes, from there on you've finally given birth to an MGTOW member. These people are the results of constantly meeting women who've just used and betrayed and drained them of their resources, money, time, whatever.

Now you can see where and how this MGTOW concept and its members come to be. It's basically men who are tired of being betrayed and drained and have finally concluded that all women are evil and no man should put up with them anymore. So basically the members and even the starters of MGTOW are men who were once the nice guys or the so called "simps", but have now faced constant heartbreaks and decided to stay and die single and unmarried. Honestly I don't blame them for turning into what they are now, frequent and constant pain to a person can either leave them mentally unstable or just turn straight cold, and from there on it's really not easy to trust anybody anymore, but like I've said before, it doesn't mean that every woman on earth is completely rotten and bad, but try convincing that to an MGTOW member, not easy.

But one question still stands though, if all these men were once the nice guys, the ones who knew or thought they knew how to treat a woman the right way is by being nice to her every time, checking on her every time and giving her all she wanted, yet still got played, then what's wrong? Why did they get betrayed and left for the guy who didn't give a damn about the woman? After all who wouldn't want to be treated nicely and taken care of, it makes us feel good doesn't it, knowing there's someone to check up on us, give something we need or want. Well, I can say this is somehow nature giving a brutal lesson to these men that being nice all the time can get you killed, figuratively speaking, let me put it this way, a wise man once said "Being too nice gets you used and being too mean pushes people away. Life is balance". I think we all know that being too nice in this society will mostly get you used and drained, and this is exactly what happened to these men, and because of this, nature had decided to remind them that this is what you get for being too nice to women. Let's be honest, having someone who's nice to you is great and all but at times it can get a little bit tiresome, I mean being a nice guy is basically like being a yes man, whenever someone says or wants something, you just acknowledge it or approve it, it can get boring at times, sure you get to enjoy the free goodies, but it won't make that person any interesting, now this is quite the reason why women who were once with these men decided to leave or just drain them of their resources yet still went for the bad boy. There's a saying that "women like adventure and being made feel special and active and someone who can be commanding and even rough at times", and I honestly don't think they can get these things from the nice guys, that's why they choose the bad boys, because they know these bad boys have these traits even though they know they're not rich or famous or even sometimes a little harsh to them, but still go back to them, because they like the adventures, sometimes they want the thrill of a man who's commanding her to do or not do something, it commands respect, but a man who's always nice won't command any respect to her, it's like him being submissive to her rather than the opposite, that's why women will easily go back to the ruffian who she knows is rough and tough.

Honestly speaking relationships are supposed to be fun, active, adventurous and getting on each other's nerves then making up for it either with sex, cuddle or whatever it is that turns some couples on, just remember to have respect for each other, that's the most important thing, but having someone that's constantly nice all the time and apologizes every single time is like having a "yes man robot", it can get boring and tiresome, that's the truth, instead of enjoying the thrill of a partner, it's like having a relationship slave, for men sure they can appreciate a nice woman because of her submissiveness, but to women, they won't exactly take it as a sign of strength from a man, but that doesn't mean a nice woman wont also get played by his man, there's always a vice versa to any story, even nice women sometimes get played and used by men who they acted nice to, it's a messed up world.

So there you have it, these men or MGTOW members are the results of being used and played because of their being too nice characters and attitudes. But you know what, that's not the only reason for this, poor selection is also the cause of turning nice guys into stone cold, what do I mean by this? Well it's nice to show some love to the person you admire but if it's the wrong person, then you're really just wasting your time and resources. Just think about it, you've met a woman, but all she's shown you is pain, regret, heart and head ache, the only time she makes you feel special is when she comes to you to ask for something, that's when she smiles at you and make you think whatever you're saying is funny, then when she finally gets it, she's gone, just by observing this don't you think it's time to pull the plug on that relationship, I get it, sometimes when someone falls in love they can really fall in love, it's like they literally become blinded by their feelings for the woman that it doesn't matter what the woman does to him, it makes no change of him loving her.

Getting broken by someone doesn't mean that every other single person you come across is going to be like that, there's someone who's going to be worthy of your effort and make you feel special, that's why there are men who I know or even you might know, were once played and used by their woman, but are now one of the happiest men after they found the right partner to commit to, don't give up hope because of a few people you ran into who seemed like heartless menaces. There's a saying that goes "There are 7 billion people in the world, so if one of them behaves badly towards you or plays you in the wrong way, they're actually doing you great favor by telling you that they're not worth your time, that means you can move on to the next 6,999,999,999 other people of which some of them may be worth your time and effort", so just because you came across the first one or two or even three women who were all negative, don't conclude by saying I'm giving up on dating and marriage because all women are the same, no my friend, they're really helping you by guiding you to the positive people for you, because the truth is that to the wrong person you mean nothing, but to the right person you mean everything. And you should know, the wrong woman for you, will make you feel like you're not enough, but to the right woman, she'll make you feel a king and see a proper worth of spoiling her with love and gifts as nothing to it. So remember proper selection is the best selection overall. As a man, any man at some point was a simp for a woman he once loved or adored, and he thought that doing everything in his will to make her happy was the best choice, yet he came to meet up with heartbreaking surprise that made him question the concept of love and relationships, and now they've turned cold and emotionless, I know some guys who've been through that and maybe you know some as well, its ok to deal with the pain, but don't convince yourself that it's the end of love for you, everybody needs love at some point, but turning yourself cold isn't pushing people away, it's just pushing you away from the ones who were even supposed to be the right one for you, some people after turning MGTOW because of their broken hearts have missed out on the opportunities to meet the best and right partner for them in their lives, but they'll never find that out now because they've decided that all women are the same and don't want to partake in any of that relationship stuff anymore, please don't let this be you.

Anyways, I think that about wraps it up on everything about MGTOW, the so called "lone-wolf" movement, like I said, everything has a good side and a bad side to it, so in whatever circumstances that gets you to choose any of these movements, it's up to you to decide which side you want to be on.

SIMPING

Now let's cover another topic concerning a term which in modern days now easily refers to a weak man or a weak woman.

To my reader, the term simp or simping may not be exactly a new term for you. It's a very common term used in relationships mostly or in just normal situations explaining someone's attitude particularly to the other gender, mostly men are termed as the simps by their fellow men or even women.

Let's digest this slowly, simp in a more rational meaning is a typical internet slang which means someone who craves or gives constant attention and excessive sympathy to someone who isn't showing or giving back the same energy or vibes, usually it's for affection or a relationship, like I said, mostly done to the other gender. What we can see nowadays in modern relationships, as I said before, really messed up nowadays, we can see many men craving to give or get excessive attention from women they like or even the other way around, a woman giving all her attention to a man she adores. A man will do anything for the woman buy everything she wants and say anything she wants, or a woman can give whatever the man wants, give him all the sex he wants, buy him whatever he needs, but the sad return is that they don't give back the same energy, now the ones doing all these stuffs are called the simps and their actions are simping. It's weird though, the word simp actually meant simpleton, which describes a stupid or foolish person, so now I'm guessing they found the perfect people to call this word.

But what actually describes the actions of a so called simp? Well, as I explained earlier the concept of being too nice to people or being a people pleaser, doing and agreeing with everything they say, want and do, that's mostly what simps do. Let's take a good example here, there's a term for men who know or think they know how to handle a woman, these men are called the "real men", and what exactly is their way of handling a woman, well that's easy, give her what she wants, she wants money for rubbish spending give it to her, she wants constant attention give it to her, she wants anything no matter how ridiculous it is, just give it to her, if she cheats on you forgive her, if she disrespects you, talk to her and make things ok, if she rejects you keep staying by her side in the hopes that she'll one day accept you, always put her on a pedestal by constantly complimenting her and make her feel special, this is what the real men do, now such men are called simps, because despite doing everything for that woman, what do they get in return, a thank you, and a kiss on the cheek, and if they're lucky even sex (but this is considered as luck for them, because the more they keep on being a real man and doing all that nice shit for them, the more that luck fades away and disappears, which means no sex).

Now that's for the men's side of simping, now let's see the women side of simping, which is really not so much different, women who are considered simps usually buy constant gifts for the guy they like, give him constant and any kind sex he wants, endure an abusive relationship because they like the guy, accept disrespect from the guy, getting hurt physically and emotionally and still enduring, forgiving the guy for cheating no matter how many times he's done, fulfilling all his desires and all that, this is women simping.

Remember what I said before. Doing all this stuff is fine, just as long as it's for the right person. Simping is actually like the man or woman has been emotionally blinded by the person they like to the extent they can't see anything wrong with being with them, whether it's being disrespected, abused, used, played, cheated, no matter what, they'll still choose to say they love that person, and it's crazy honestly, I've actually witnessed women being beaten by their men to the extent of almost suffocating, yet still ran back to the same guy, and I've even witnessed men being publicly disrespected by their women and even used and drained of their resources and energy yet still went back to the same woman and apologized to them for not being perfect, the man apologizing, not the woman.

I understand that falling in love sometimes can actually mean "Falling in love" and literally becoming blind by your affections for that person, but there are times in a relationship or in life generally where you need to stop following your heart and listen to what your brain is telling you, you need to have what's best for you and not just settle for what you think is good enough.

I don't mean to sound rude, but honestly giving all that vibe and energy to someone who doesn't even match with your levels is certain pain, just imagine doing all that for a man or woman and not getting anything in return, it's like enslaving yourself and getting disrespected like a street dog. Honestly, this simping stuff is really bad, if I may say so it's even degrading, and according to the meaning of the word, these people are foolish, I mean this is just causing you to lose your self-respect as man or woman. Even on the internet we can see lots of people explaining that men need to stop simping to women, this issue seems like it's common to men more than women, though it does happen to women too, but like I said before, nowadays women want to be the one on top, so no wonder simping is more common to men, anyways, all these videos on the internet explaining how men simp to women and why they should stop simping are actually there because it's a drastically growing theme on today's men, because we are now living in an era where men are honestly becoming feminine, weaker, lazier and even less ambitious, so no wonder it's easy for them to submit to a woman's control, as I said at the beginning, men back then were more ambitious and had their careers and futures planned ahead of them and that's why they weren't easily driven by emotions or women. So basically what these men on the internet with their anti-simping videos are trying to do, is basically showing and explaining that men aren't supposed to be like the way they are now. Other videos just explain how men should stop simping because most of the women they're actually simping for nowadays aren't worth it, and they may be right, just look at it, with the constant rise of over controlling women, and OnlyFans stars, who would want to simp or submit to such women, I wouldn't, but surprisingly there are men who actually submit to these kind of women, take for instance the OnlyFans models subscribers, they literally pay a lot of money just to get naked pictures of girls online, and even boast about being the most spender on the girl's account page, tell me if that's not simping.

And for the women, let's look at how the tables shift here. We can see, mostly modern days now how women are more attracted and submissive to the naughty or so called bad boy, no matter how abusive, bad or dangerous they are, the women still simp for them. Here, if the man wants money, the girl will do anything just to get it for him, if the man wants sex, it's just a matter of seconds for the girl to give it to him, if the man cheats on the girl with another girl, the simp girl will forgive him, even if it's more than twice, if the man won't check in on the girl even if she's sick, not a problem for the girl, but when he wants his desires fulfilled, it's a no problem for the girl, even if the man won't pick up any phone calls or answer any messages from the girl, it's all ok for the girl. Like I said, its literally enslaving yourself to someone who doesn't even give a shit about you. This is what simping is on the women's side.

But you know, one question got me thinking, why do people simp? There's clearly someone who's right for you and who's willing to treat you better and make you the happiest person ever, yet still why do they go back to the wrong people? That's one question that itched my mind for a while until I found out something. If you look at it, most of the men that tend to simp for these women, are usually the ones who are sometimes known as the nerds, the guys who don't know how to talk to women, the guys who are mostly inexperienced with women, that's why in almost all of the videos on the internet that teach men on how to stop simping to women, one of the most common things they teach is to talk to more women, go outside and talk to more girls, because the more you hangout around girls, talk to them and getting rejected, the more you get to know and understand girls and the more confident you become, because honestly, just look at the situation where a man has to pay a ton of money just to talk to an OnlyFans model, a literal online girl, when there are a ton of beautiful girls outside, you're actually paying to chat with a girl and get her naked pictures, what for? That's really weird, the people that do these kind of stuff are mostly the ones who spend most of their days locking themselves inside and just playing and paying on their computers, I don't think you'll find these characters on a person who continuously goes outside to different places and talks to different girls, no matter if he's getting rejected or what, no, you won't find such characters, because he knows how women act, react and behave, thus his building up his game and confidence to get more beautiful girls, who, he won't even have to spend a dime or a penny on just to get them or talk to. So this is basically the most reason as to why men simp for girls, first of all, it's the lack of experience of not talking to enough girls and locking yourself inside like a caged monkey, second, it's the fear of talking women. Now this might be a bit underrated, but the truth is that men are scared of approaching women and talking to them. I used to wonder why it's like that, I mean they're just normal people too, it's not like they're aliens or anything, then what's the matter? And that's when it hit me, the fear of being rejected, when approaching a woman, what does a man actually intend to do, well ask for her number, ask her on a date out, ask her to be his girlfriend, ask her to marry him, but that all narrows down to the questions like "what if she says no, what if I say something stupid, what if she's not interested, what if I make fun of myself in front of her, what if she doesn't have the same feelings for me", and that's when the man decides to back off and go back to locking himself up. Truth is, every man is afraid of talking to a girl because of the exact same reasons and worries as you have, but heck, they do it anyways, remember, practice makes perfect, as you go on talking to more and more girls, you'll soon start to get better at it and step up your game and know exactly what to say and act around the next girl you meet. Just imagine it like you're called for a job interview, you don't know if you'll actually get the job or not, yet you still prep up and dress up and go anyways, and even if you don't get the job, you don't worry about it because there are tons of other places to apply for, and that rejection didn't make you sick or explode or anything, you came out knowing where your wrongs were and went on to the other job interview, so just do it, the best she can say is no, and you'll still live, you may never know, the first shot may be the only shot you need to land a smoking hot woman who's right for you my friend.

And what about the women, why do they simp? This may be somehow relevant to what I said, I said men with more experience and confidence around girls are the ones who usually tend to attract more females to them. So women are actually attracted to the bad boys because mostly of the traits they have, which is confidence, the abundance mentality, what is the abundance mentality you may ask. Well picture it this way, you're fishing in a lake and you miss one fish, what do you do? Pack up your fishing net and head home? No! you trigger it again to catch another one, because you're not worried with infinite number of fish in the lake. That's how bad boys are like, they don't care if one girl says no, because they know there are tons of other beautiful girls out there who are waiting to be approached, and once girls start to see this level of confidence and mindset in a man, they start to wonder why he didn't bother to convince her anymore, after all, it's obvious that women want attention, so if they don't get it from a certain man and see that he doesn't even mind it, they start to wonder what special thing does this guy have to know he can just attract another woman, is he famous or popular? Is he rich? Is he good in bed? These are the questions that run through the girl's mind, and after noticing this, they don't want to pass on whatever the man has which may seem attractive and she decides to try whatever is necessary to get him back, no matter the resources, no matter the time, no matter the sex, hence the simping starts here, though sometimes it doesn't end well after ending up in the arms of the wrong man, abusive or just uses her and in the end starts to miss having just a regular guy.

So in my opinion, this is honestly as to why people simp, and despite having all these online teachers and videos explaining and criticizing how simping is a terrible thing, there are honesty still ignorant people who choose to continue simping to the guy or girl, because they believe that this is the only way to treat them in order to get what they want, a relationship, sex or whatever it is they want from them. But what are the outcomes of this? What happens after simping for so long, yet still not getting the girl or guy or not getting sex, I honestly don't want to believe that someone can continuously simp for 20, 30, 50 years and on, there has to be a breaking point, and that breaking point is, whether a guy is simping for a girl, the girl eventually gets married to another guy or continuously sleeps around with other guys apart from the simp following her around. And what of the simp girl following the guy around, well the guy will usually sleep around with other girls and cheat often until the simp girl can't take no more. From these simp girls and boys is where we get the birth of men and women who you hear say "all women are the same, emotionless, heartless monsters" and "all men are dogs, the only thing they want is sex!", now I don't think this is what they would be saying if they had found the right person.

Honestly, nobody chooses to simp or be a simp, they're just doing what the heart tells them to do, that's why I said sometimes you have to listen to your brain more than your heart, because the heart can be deceiving at times, why do you think there's the saying "listen to what your mind is telling you", or "trust your gut instincts", you might be thinking there's a saying "follow your heart", true there's that, but in what situation or context should you follow it, you can't expect to follow your heart that's telling you to forgive and continue loving the girl who's constantly sleeping around with other men and disrespects you while you're paying for everything, or you can't possibly still want to be with a man who cheats on you, over and over again and abuses you like some kind of slave or sex doll, I don't think anyone would actually follow their hearts in this kind of situation, but if there are those that still do, then God be with you and see where it takes you from there.

So essentially, simping is a terrible thing to do, it's just like being too nice to someone but in an overly affectionate manner, so please men, stop simping for the wrong woman, and women, stop simping for the wrong guy, why do I keep on emphasizing the wrong person? Because your attention matters, you keep giving and giving more while the other person just takes and takes to the point you feel drained yourself and have nothing left, while the girl or guy doesn't care, you keep trying to make everything workout for you two, but whatever mistake happens, you feel like it's your fault and feel like it's your obligation to make everything alright again, but just remember one thing, in the end, if all goes bad, no matter how much you complain of all that you did for the other person , they'll still say they never asked you to do any of that for them, and you know what, they're right, first of all, the fact of being a simp just means that you've blocked yourself from using the word "NO" to the person you're simping for, if he or she wants something, you give it to her, buying them crazy and expensive gifts even when they didn't ask for it, just imagine the simp girl buying gifts for the guy who doesn't actually care for her even to check on her, gives him every kind of sex he wants, uses her money to spend on him loses her time for him, if he has a debt, you use up your savings to help him clear it, he cheats several times and just because you caught him and he apologizes for it, you forgive him and hope things might get better now, yet in the end he checks out another girl, and even if you complain you used all your time for him and degraded yourself like a sex puppet for him just remember, he never asked you to do any of that for him, and even if he did, just look at the signs in your relationship if it's worth doing what he's asked for or wants, you can either say no or continue being blinded by the slave love you have for him.

And just look at what the simp men are doing, the girl wants money, they give her more than she asked for, her birthday's coming up, they find the craziest and most expensive gift of all, she wants to go out with her friends, he pays for everything and doesn't even get an invite, the simp guy pays for everything, her insurance, bills, shopping, medical bills, outings, rent bill to the house or apartment of which she's going to bring another dude to sleep with while the simp gets told to go outside, finally in the end when the simp's mind comes back to him and realizes that he's wasted all his time, money and other potential resources and still got treated like a slave boy puppet and the girl eventually ends up with some other dude or married to someone else, he starts complaining to her and saying "I did everything for you, I paid all your expenses, I wasted all my money on you", true, you did all that, but her answer is just going to be "I never asked you to do any of that for me" and you know she's right about that, because you had the choice to say no or you don't have what she wanted, but yet you still chose to play the comic book hero.

And you know, you can't really blame the people getting all those special treatment and gifts, because come on, what human wouldn't want free gifts and surprises.

So there you have it folks, this is the art of simping, so please, do what is right and stop degrading yourself.

GENDER VALUES

Values, this is where the odds define all odds. Each gender has its own values, but what does this mean? We'll take a look at everything value based in each gender, what values do men have and when exactly does that value begin to sprout? And what values do women have and when does it also begin and when does it end? You see everything has its limits, values just like any other thing, has its start and end, how long your values maintain depends mainly on what you do to keep and maintain it.

Are you rich? That's a value, are you knowledgeable? That's a value, are you skillful? That's a value. Anything you possess and can use it to provide back to the society is a value. But does that mean then as long as you don't have any of these things, you're what valueless? Well let's see then.

First of all, have you ever heard of the saying "A woman's value is like milk, it rots early, and a man's value is like wine, it stays for a long time"? If not, then this is specifically what we're going to discuss here, and to some readers, this may seem unfair or incorrect, but honestly it's the hard truth, because whether you accept it or not, the truth will always remain the truth and a lie will always remain a lie. Like I said before, both men and women have their own values, and each value according to society today is measured on what they can bring or provide to the society or just in a basic relationship.

So does that mean that everyone is born with a value? Well honestly, No! because as soon as a man or woman is born, you're just a kid, you're the one who's supposed to be looked after, taken care of, given whatever you want or cry for, but when a certain age reaches where the tables turn and it's now your turn to give back just like you've been taking all those years, but regarding to men and women it's a bit different here, and the difference particularly starts at a certain age, for the women more specifically starts at the teenage years, according to research done, teachers and even philosophers, a woman's age of value starts at 18 or even 16 and goes straight towards her 30s, this is why women during their college years or teen years are able to attract a lot of men and termed as "college baddies, hot teens" and whatever term there is, but according to society now, they have to give something right? Well not conditionally, just think about it, these teenager girls have a higher chance of getting married or getting into a relationship at this age, because they're beautiful, they're full charisma, they're full of aura, they're energetic, it's like fresh fish out of water, some even say they're better in bed, but that's for you to complement.

Well does that mean it's enough for them to be considered valuable? The answer is yes, because every man likes a fresh, young, beautiful girl either to engage in a relationship or marry, so rationally, women's values are measured by the society in terms of their looks and charm, no wonder they have little time to enjoy it. Honestly speaking, women can get away with their looks at this teen age, they can find a rich, good looking, muscular guy to settle with, and at some percentage it happens, but, the value of this beauty and charm they have starts to fade away as soon as they reach the age of 30s and above, because that's when most of the makeup won't even be able to hide wrinkles and oldness on their faces, and this value will drastically fade away depending on what they used to do at their prime time, were they humble and submissive, did they conceal their sexuality or just give it away to random men like passing flyers at a public park, were they full of humility or wild party girls, were they drinking and smoking or did they have self-respect and religiously moral? What these girls do or did in their prime has a significant effect on their later years, mentally, health wise, emotionally, even physically, just look at it in today's society women who've been through a lot of shit in their prime are now facing the consequences, they're termed as aunties because of promiscuity and old age, you should know that constant and frequent sex even just for fun can cause mild aging, scientifically proven, don't believe me, do the research and try it out yourself, over and over and over again, you can literally get skinny and pale from doing this, and this is what's happening to the girls who used to fool around with their bodies, now time is fooling around with their taste, the girls who jumped from one guy to the other like a pogo stick are now facing emotion unsettlement, they refuse to believe that a man can be loyal, they think all what men want is sex, well if that's what you've been showing people for years and years, don't blame the next guy who comes at you for sex, you get what you deserve, apart from that, these girls who refused to settle in their prime are mostly the ones who are now hunting for married men, because they see their fellow women who settled are now married, and because they didn't and are now labelling themselves as single and searching, for so long they have carried that title and now decided to cling to a married man.

The women that used to smoke and drink aren't even approached by men, because I don't think a man would want a future with a woman who smokes and gets drunk, even the smoking girls now have their own title, they're called "dragons", seriously! Everything has a name nowadays. But this is the hard truth, just look at the women who used to be humble and obedient and knew how to conceal themselves, a large number of them are married to a wealthy, looking guy, and look at the women who were, well, promiscuous, naughty, party goers and all that stuff, they're literally trying to survive the day with one or two meals. But all this could be avoided by considering what's really important in your prime years, and this is the truth, and just remember, as time and age goes up and up, your value goes down and down and may end up as the creepy cat lady or the single auntie who isn't married to anyone yet is a single mother to one or many kids, that's how unfair life is.

You can even see the number of girls who are virgins nowadays is drastically low, I'm not saying there aren't any virgins left, but let's be real, it's like finding a needle in a haystack, a one out of ten girls nowadays will tell you they're virgins, and the rest, well, just be ready to hear their body count.

By the way, just in case you were wondering what being promiscuous means or what body count is. Well simply, promiscuous is not having restrictions with how many sexual partners you can have, two, three, ten, twenty, that's all you, if you can handle it that is, a perfect example of the Round Table theory I talked about earlier. And what about body count, well in a normal dictionary it just means the number of people killed in a war or disaster, but in the new era, it means the number of people someone had sexual relations with, so if its few men a girl has slept with, then it's a low body count, but if it's a lot of men, then that's a high body count, this can apply to both men and women, but in today's society, its normally used on women. Both these terms have taken part a large discussion in modern day societies in the digital era, women now are termed promiscuous because there's literally no stop to how many men she can lay with, and the number of how many she has laid with is what you'll get as the body count.

But then, how about the men? What about their value? As I said before, nobody is born with value, at a certain age is where your value starts to appear, for girls, we've seen their value is mostly based on their looks, and what about the men then? Well, at the age of 18 to 30, the teenage years, men respectfully have no value, why? Because on the basis of men, they're the providers, and at the age of 18s to 30 let's be honest, it's the age when a man is in high school, college, looking for a job or probably an intern or beginner at his job, they can't fully give back or provide to the society, and men need to have a certain status or lifestyle or occupation to be considered as valuable, like I said before, are you rich, or knowledgeable? At the age of 30s and above is when men have finally started to build themselves from the ground up, making money, a job, build a house, buy a car, prepare for marriage, invest wisely, start a business, just so they can give back to the society, but if you're from 18s to the 30 age just know people won't see you as valuable even if you're a straight 'A' student in college, if they stand you besides a man in his 40s who's rich and seen a lot of the world, who do you think society will listen to most? That's for you to answer.

So technically, men's values start from his 30s going up, because this is the age that people see he's old enough, may have some sort of experience on the streets and if you have a job, that respect may earn a little boost because you now have some money to even pay taxes and be considered as an adult, and let me tell you, that value will keep on going up, the more a man builds himself, mentally, physically, in terms of wealth and richness, he's value will keep going up and up, unlike women who time has done an unfair chess game on them. As men keep improving themselves, so does their value and worth keep rising, and you know, it won't even matter how promiscuous the man is, as long as he has all that stuff, people won't care, because valuable people can get away with anything, just look around, all these stars, artists, celebrities and famous people, no matter how many women they sleep with, no one can judge them, because they have what society wants.

That's why there's the saying that goes like "Nature is unfair to men, while Time is unfair to women". You can see here as long as men can't provide anything, then they're nothing, and as long as women's beauty fades away with time, then no one will want a middle aged lookalike woman. This is the hard truth of the society. If a man who has no job, no money, no looks, but somehow manages to go out with a beautiful, young and sexy girl, people are going to say she's way out of his league, and when a woman who's past her prime goes out with a rich, smart, good-looking, successful man, people are going to say she's not right for him, he deserves someone better, younger, more beautiful. Time and nature have really flipped the tables here on both genders.

But what about the teenagers of this century who can easily be millionaires by the time they're 19 or 20 years of age? Let's admit it, times have changed, we live in a time where things are much different as they were back then with our grandparents, there are online businesses, YouTube, digital marketing, freelancing and all that other stuff, so are these young girls and boys also considered to be valuable? The direct answer is, Yes, like I said, the only thing society cares about now is your value, what you have, what you can give, so if you're 19 and a millionaire, then you've got society's respect, I think we can openly see this, young artists, actors or entrepreneurs whether 19, 20, 24 whatever, yet are seen dating beautiful girls like models, fashion or brand ambassadors who are 30, 32 whatever, and nobody complains about the age difference, because as soon as they see the headlines like "19 year old millionaire dating 31 year super model", they'll just focus on the millionaire part, the rest doesn't matter. And I guess this works both ways, today we can even see women who are even aged 50, 54, who are millionaires, yet dating young men who are 24, 25, maybe because of the good looks, or their charming essence or whatever it is they were attracted to, and still nobody will say anything, sure you can judge in silence, but no one can stand up to the millionaire, and besides, stuff like that is getting normalized every day of our lives.

So regarding values, you need to have these society necessities to be known as a man or a woman, but you know what society can't take away, the fact despite that you may not have a job or be rich or not the most attractive man in the room, you're still a man, having or not having all that won't take away the fact that if you still walk down the street, or sit somewhere, people are still going to see you as a man. And for the girls, despite the fact that you're past your prime, or how old you are, you're still going to be seen as a woman. I'm saying this because, in regards to what is going on these days and how crazy people have become to get what they know society wants, things are really getting out of control, I mean just look around, a lot of women nowadays, the slightest amount of money they get, they spend it on plastic surgery to try and get back the youths they think they've lost, facial reconstruction, lip enhancement, jawline surgery, eye surgery, and all that nonsense just to look young again, because they know that as long as their youth is gone, no man is going to want them anymore and they won't get fancy compliments anymore, and if that's not enough, they'll result to butt and breast implants to result to other methods of getting what they want, if you catch my drift, but just remember those pills, injections, stitches and balloons won't work forever, sooner or later they'll all drain and reveal the real you, which to women in reality will end in humility and shame, I think we can see that to all the girls who undergo all these operations, most of them end in disasters, cancer, some get blind, intense pain in their areas, and sometimes even death. So please just stick to originality, even though your age is past, that's still you, everything will come to you at the perfect time, it's all a matter of taking care of yourselves on your early stage.

As for the men, there's a saying nowadays "Another man down", a lot of men now are turning from their straight gender into gays (transgender), some believe by becoming a woman, it can be simplified for them to get money or even getting married by a rich man, this is really sickening, or some do it just for the fame and attraction to become a celebrity or a star. Basically, these men think by being a woman it's easy to succeed by just selling their bodies for money, to them I can acknowledge the term that they are weak and foolish men. Sure society has a high demand for success from men, but it doesn't mean to go through humiliating and grotesque process, apart from that, others have resulted to stealing, killing, robbing, even witchcraft if I may say so, look, just look at the men who already are successful in the right way, they too were in your position, didn't know what to do, where to go, but despite all that, they never quit, and eventually their opportunities showed up just the right time. And besides, taking a shortcut will always end horribly, sure you can steal, make yourself a woman, but before you do, think of the consequences, you could get killed, abandoned even humiliated, is that all really worth it just to get money the quick way just to impress society, sometimes you have to value your own self-worth instead of going harm's way.

So, now that we've seen what the values of each gender are and how they play their parts in society today, and even in the past eras. My advice to the women and men struggling to get their values in shape is, always remember your worth first, sure you need money to live, but that doesn't mean losing your worth and self-respect along with it, there's a saying "Never trade respect for attention", work hard and put in the work, consistency and patience are the primary keys for success for a valuable man who knows his worth. Also, don't go to horrible lengths to deny who you are as a woman, just because you believe you're past your pride years doesn't mean you will never get married or achieve anything for that matter, for the women who are still in their prime (18, 20, 22, 24 etc.), these are the most important years for you to stabilize yourself and build your boundaries and respect, in short stop being promiscuous, stop normalizing the hot teen girl summer vibe, stop drinking, smoking and all other abominable things out there, because it may seem fun at first on your enjoyment years, but the outcomes of doing all this will cost you a lot.

The other thing is to be careful with what kind of friends you choose and invite into your life, because the other thing I've noticed is that most of these bad behaviors done by women and wrong actions taken by men are the influence of most of the friends we hang out with in our lives. It's actually a shame these days that there might be a girl who has self-respect, doesn't normalize having body counts, doesn't wear cloth that reveal most of her body, doesn't drink or smoke, and is even a virgin, but because of the type of company she keeps and calls them her friends who normalize all that nasty stuff, majority beats minority, they influence her to start doing all that, "Come on girl, you're still a virgin you're wasting your precious youth, let's go to the party and get wasted a little, it's the only life you've got, drink a little it'll make you feel better, you need to go to the club, you'll get a man there", all these are what her idiotic friends tell her to do, and because she calls them her friends , she doesn't want to disappoint and joins the group, that's one of the major ways a good girl is lost, though sometimes it could be the jealousy among women, I mean, if a non-virgin girl sees a girl who's still a virgin or doesn't ruin her body, she thinks just because she's lost her way, why not mess up someone else's way, she doesn't want to seem the only one used up.

Even the men who mistakenly trust the wrong people, I know there's the spirit of brotherhood, but there are times you need to use your brain and not let your friend's brain plan what you should do or not do, in times when men are facing difficulties, there comes a time where the man seems like he would do anything to get what he wants, that's when the misleading friends come in, "Look bro, life is hard now, there are no other means, stealing that money will be easy as pie and no one will find out, your family is depending on you, sacrifices need to be made, some people need to die for the sake of others, they've already had their fun of money, now it's time they gave it up", I don't think you'll hear this kind of stuff from friends who want the best for you, or when you're sitting alone.

So remember, values are important, but just don't lose yourself or your worth trying to maintain it.

ATTRACTIONS

On the issue of attractions, we'll take a look at what are the needs and wants of the other gender, I mean what do women find attractive in men, is it money, good looks, status, confidence or something else? And what do men find attractive in women, is it a big chest, big butt (maybe that's the reason for latest increase in constant butt surgery and implants), beauty or what is it?

Everybody's got something they're attracted to on the opposite gender, such attractions though can be narrowed down to wants and needs. You want a man who's very rich, but is that what you actually need though? You want a woman who's got a big butt, but is that what you really need in a woman?

I'm not going to lie though, with the constant rise of social media, globalization and societal changes, now it's like people don't even know what they actually need in a partner, what they're actually attracted to. Look at it this way, a woman who constantly scrolls through social media like Instagram and sees other women getting spoiled by her man with money, cloths, luxury cars, or sees a woman who prides herself and shows off her man who has a gym bod or a big chest, what do you think is going to be the outcome of this? Easy, the woman watching and admiring all these is also going to want that same kind of treatment and the same kind of man with the same physical features, which is one of the ways people get misled and think that is what they want, when in reality it's not what they need. Or a man who scrolls the internet or adult sites performing stunt related sex scenes and constantly sees women with big butts and a big chest, no matter if it's an implant or what, or sees other men posting pictures and videos of their women who have big butts or a curvy shape, what' going to happen? Exactly the same, he's also going to want a woman with all the curves and the butt and the chest and everything, but actually it's not what he needs in a partner. Both of these people of different gender have one thing in common, they both got their assumptions of attractiveness from the media, they think what they see is what is good, just because they see those other people posting all that stuff and are happily married or in relationship, they start to assume if they had the same things, they would also be happy, when in reality it's not true. This is why sometimes I like to term social media as curation bias, in case you don't know what that means, it's when there's a selective presentation of information where only the good side is shown and the bad side is omitted, this is actually done a lot on social media in our society today, most people tend to show only the highlight of their lives, the travelling, the money, the luxury everything expensive, but in real life that's all fake, and I think you've witnessed some people who got exposed as being someone who was not actually who they were while highlighting their lives on the media, fake gurus, fake billionaires, fake tech experts, fake influencers and all those others.

This has seriously misled a lot of people into believing as soon as they have what they see, then they'll be happy, wrong! Social media and society has messed up your mind and even your beliefs. As a woman you have to differentiate what you want in a man and what you need as a woman, you may want a man who's rich and successful, sure you get him, but he's abusive, rarely cares for you, all he cares is his money and expensive things, never has time for you or never shows any compassion, is that really worth having in your life? But in today's life as wicked as it is, I wouldn't be surprised if some women say yes, as long as she gets the dough.

And as man you have to know what you need in a woman versus what you want as a man, you want a girl with big butts, fine you got her, but all she does is cause drama and fighting and never brings anything supportive in your life to the extent some men even start going for therapy sessions, well you did want a big butt girl right? Well there you have it, now you have to deal with whatever comes along with it.

Look, there's nothing wrong with wanting a man who's rich and good looking, and I understand a man may want a woman who has a nice looking body, it's like human nature, women are designed to look for the best quality and men are just attracted to what they see, that's why you can see a woman may date a man who's rich yet still cheat with the garbage disposal man just because he has something different, and even men who can go out with a woman who's curvaceous and most beautiful, yet still cheat with a slim girl who's normal looking, why? Because it's what they thought they wanted but not what they actually needed.

Let me clarify things a bit here, as I explained earlier, women are care takers and nurtures, not providers or protectors, so they need a man who can protect and provide for them and most importantly love them intimately. And men are the providers and protectors, so they need a woman who can nurture and take care of him and his family. But instead of that, people are now deranged by big butts and expensive lifestyle, because you're upsetting the natural balance of order. The wrong attractions because of the wrong wants can lead to the wrong outcomes, nowadays women tend to choose men who have the expensive lifestyle, no matter whether his married or what, they see the money, the good life, they want it and will do anything to get it without considering the consequences, the results aren't exactly appealing, they end up in the arms of a man who's abusive or just use them as a sex toy, a man who's violent, a man who doesn't give a damn about her, soon she starts regretting the choices she made of going out with the guy. And men who tend to want women with big butts and beauty and an attractive chest also tend to face some horrible outcomes, they start complaining that the woman is unbelievably dirty, literally provides no mental, emotional or even spiritual support or doesn't offer anything in the relationship besides demanding a luxurious and expensive lifestyle that the man soon won't be able to afford anymore.

And because of the crazy wants people have nowadays to the opposite gender, it has given birth to some serious uncanny tragedies, like what you may ask! Because it's obviously known that men nowadays want women with big butts, maybe even the rich ones, women now run straight to the plastic surgeon's office, increase their butt size, their breast size, get a bigger curve, fix and beautify their faces with eyelashes and lips, without regarding the consequences of these actions, they think having all this stuff is what will attract men their way, even the ones they want, if that's true, then why are majority of these women with all this stuff still single, not married, single mothers, living alone and whatever man comes their way just wants the pleasure of using them and leaving? Because it's not what men actually need.

Apart from that, men have now realized that women want men who are rich, thus result to commit heinous crimes, men who have muscular physique, instead of hitting the gym, get body surgery to enhance muscle mass, which mostly ends up in a disaster, or just use body enhancement drugs, men who have certain inches of their private parts, again result to get enhancement surgery or drugs, leading their lives to overdependence of these drugs, but if it's actually what women want, then why do the women who have a rich man tend to cheat with the man who's a regular guy even a fast food employee just because he makes her laugh, or even cheat with guy who doesn't give her the time of day, or if they get a muscular physique guy, they tend to cheat with guy with a dad bod? It's not the basis of want, it's the principle of need.

With that said, it's clearly seen we are living in a time where most people don't really understand how the laws of attraction work. And the few people who do know how they work, are the ones who don't stress what to do to attract the right partner. And what's even more strange is that there are coaches or even influencers on social media teaching people how to attract, there are now principles that men and women are being instructed to follow to attract the girl or guy they want, they'll teach stuff like "If you want to get a girl who's a 10/10, you need to wear certain cloths, put on certain perfume, walk and talk in a certain manner, shave your hair or beard in a certain way, when you get her number don't text her immediately, don't seem too desperate, show her you have options, always dress smart, focus on her red flags and green flags, be interesting and adventurous", can someone really keep this all up and maintain that lifestyle for so long? I wonder.

And what principles do girls get tutored to attract the guy they think they want? "Be a baddie, play with the nice guy, hookup with a toxic guy, promiscuity helps her get the right guy, going to the club will get you higher chances of getting the right man, a poor man will provide nothing for you, don't make it seem like you're interested in him, don't make it too easy for him, always make him pay for all your expenses because he's the man", and so on and so on, it's like a daily routine women now have to follow just because they think it's the way of getting the man they want hooked on them.

It's really a shame nowadays that in love, relationships and marriages people have to adhere to certain conducts, attitudes and behaviors, I mean seriously, do all that stuff just to get someone you're in love with, someone once told me "there is no champion in love", I don't know about those flirting experts though, maybe those guys have it all figured out, but I know some serious Casanova teachers who were sometimes even considered role models to the people in teaching them about love and marriages and all that stuff, but even they fell into the hole of divorce and heart break, the result of being too nice or being too toxic or too masculinity I guess. Seriously though, nowadays you can't compare modern love to the old-fashioned love back then when our parents were hooking up, but someone will tell you "its modern times, everyone's doing it, we can't live like the past, that's outdated". But if that's true then answer me this, why is it that old-fashioned relationships from our parents and grandparents are still thriving to date? Yet in our so-called modern relationships, it's a blessing to get past one month of being boyfriend and girlfriend and even a bigger blessing to get past a year in marriage without one of the partners complaining and demanding a divorce.

Truth be told, attractions aren't something you force or try to imitate, they happen naturally, there are people who are attracted to weird things at times, there are men attracted to women with dimples or big bright eyes, there are women who are attracted to men with big eyebrows or bright nails. You may get the person you want just because they have the things that you want, but they get attracted to someone else who doesn't even have half of what the first one had.

Take it like this, a woman got a man who's rich and it's what she wanted, but ends up cheating with an average Joe just because he makes her feel special and makes her laugh, that's why sometimes in arguments between a man and a woman, women will sometimes say things like "I cheated on you with someone because he makes me feel special, because he makes me happy all the time, all you care about is your money and running your businesses, you never have any time for me", or even the men will say things like "I cheated on you with someone because she brings me peace, she doesn't disrespect me, she cares about how I'm doing, when was the last time you gave me sex?" and all that stuff.

And both of these are the same people that wanted a rich and successful man and a big butt beautiful woman and eventually got what they wanted, but then why all the complaints and arguments? It's what they wanted but not what they actually needed. Honestly, attractions mostly happen unexpectedly, like I said, you can't force attractions or want something and act like you're attracted to it (you may be attracted to it, but you're attracted to it in terms of lust). Then how does the unexpected attraction happen? Well, have you ever heard of love at first sight? that's a clear example of attraction, he may not be the richest person in the room or the most handsome, yet still a girl is attracted to him just because of something or a certain vibe he has, and she may not be the prettiest girl in the room or the thickest one, but something about her has got the man strangely attracted to her.

Whether you know it or not or believe it or not, there's always someone who can't keep their eyes off you and even you might not know what you got to make them stare at you. Have you ever heard girls sometimes say things like "there's just something about him that I can't keep my eyes off, the way he talks so slow and soothing, he dresses so simple, he's always minding his own business and likes to stay alone, he just seems so interesting, he looks like he really understands or knows how to treat someone, he's such a man of God" or things like that, or even men saying things like "that girl looks really cool, she just seems so down to earth, she's not trying to fit in, I like her smile or her blue eyes, the way she's religious is so nice" and stuff like that, now that is called attraction, the first glimpse you see and you're not having dirty thoughts like how big her butt is or expectations like how big is his bank account. This is how the law of attraction works, though some people don't seem to understand it and prefer chasing after their own desires.

So before you think that you don't have the money or looks to attract women, just remember there's always someone who's got their eyes fixed on you just the way you are. And before you judge yourself that you're not the thickest or the prettiest girl ever, there's always a guy who can't stop thinking of ways on how he's going to approach you. Trust me, you'll notice all this, because once attraction takes place, then comes feelings, and we all know feelings can't be hidden no matter how hard we try to hide them.

To finish this altogether, attractions are a natural state of our human bodies, we can't deny or hide from them, no matter how cold you may pretend to be. You're attracted to a white guy or a black guy, that's fine, you're attracted to a young, white slim girl, that's fine too. The important thing to remember is just make sure the one you're attracted to, reciprocates the same energy, because if they don't and you keep forcing the one sided lane of love, in the end you're going to think love is bitter and cruel, when in reality, it's all the outcomes of your poor choice of a lover guided by your own lust of attractions.

THE INFLUENCE OF SOCIAL MEDIA

Social media in my perspective is where it all began. Looking at how a large number of people are living nowadays will make you realize just how a big of an influence social media has on our society, people are seriously living the digital lifestyle today, because its where they spend most of their time throughout the entire day, I understand there are those with online businesses and its where their source of income comes from, they're fine, but mostly the youth age today spend literally the whole day scrolling through their phones looking at their role models, whether musical artists, actors and whoever else they like to follow.

Today, kids and teenagers are actually copying what they see on social media, what they see their role models doing, do I need to talk about the weird and promiscuous clothing, the habits or attitude and more. From all this we are now living with different subgroups of people, as if different religions and cultures weren't enough, we now have people characterized into cultures by their habits, appearances, mindsets and more, we'll touch on all this one bit at a time, because social media has really given birth to some seriously crazy stuff and even more crazy people.

I remember a quote from a great philosopher named Noam Chomsky, where he said "If I had to choose between government and media as the greater threat to democracy, I would choose media, because media is far more powerful in terms of shaping public perception and opinion". From this great quote, he saw what power social media had on people today, just look around, the majority of people living in our society are literally living a digital life, online dating, online sex, I wouldn't be surprised if there were even online marriages, posting a luxurious lifestyle of cars and houses while you're just actually in your parent's basement, protesting against the government and speaking out through twitter while sitting on a couch inside eating junk food, seeing what your favorite artists are up to, liking their pictures while they get paid for you to do that, while you're still borrowing money from your parents to buy you the phone to do all that, creating fake classes teaching people about particular skills while you're actually bamboozling them. It's obvious how social media has managed to take hold of everyone's mind, the new era of digital zombies, bumping into each other has never been so easy as everyone you pass by today has their head tilt down on their phones chatting or even sexting with their boyfriends or girlfriends whom they have never even met in real life.

Unfortunately, thanks to social media, we now have the tribes of, Baddies, 304s, Sigma males (or people who want to be sigma males), Alpha males, Red and Green flaggers, Dating experts and Coaches, Thirst trap gym girls, Masculine women and Feminine men and Digital Dating Subculture. All these subcultures and tribes have rose and come up thanks to social media, and somehow managed to take control of everyone's mind both men and women and impacting their relationships and marriages. Just look at it, women are doing and becoming what they see on social media, same goes for men, they're also doing and becoming what they also see and taught on social media. Women get their influence from the girls they see while scrolling, likewise men get their influence from who they listen to while also scrolling.

So how have these subcultures influenced both of these genders negatively or positively (if there is any positive side to it)? Let's start with the Baddies subculture, this tribe in particular is a major influence on the women today. Another well-known term for this are the "Slay queens". What do they do? Well, they slay, just as the name suggests. Baddies are the group of girls we commonly see while scrolling social media, particularly Instagram, how they dress, how they look, how they walk, the locations they take all their pictures from.

A baddie can be seen as a girl who flaunts a rich and successful lifestyle of expensive houses, hotels and cars, to make it look to other women viewing that she has made it while the woman viewing is just a loser. Remember when I said social media can be curation bias, this is it, baddies only show what they want other people, particularly their fellow women to see, because in all honesty, women are jealous of each other, I know jealousy is a common trait, but to women it's a bit too much. So baddies actually flaunt this kind of lifestyle to make them feel and look superior and make other women watching feel like they're nothing and even sometimes make men feel upset and embarrassed seeing that a woman has made it successfully in life, while the man doesn't even have a job yet. And it actually works, because as soon as the viewers see this, they start to desire all that, without actually knowing what's on the other side of the screen. Just a sincere question here, do you actually believe that all those baddies you see on social media actually own all that stuff they flaunt or if they actually do any hard work to get that stuff? The correct answer is NO!

Without hiding anything, most of those baddie girls you see are really just hard pretenders, some of them are really just, in a simpler term "prostitutes", yes these girls you see flexing and slaying own not even a quarter of those expensive things they flaunt, behind all of that is either a sugar daddy at work who owns everything or just one of her male clients staying at a nice hotel or something and that's when she decides to take a picture of every piece of that luxury and flex it on Instagram, thereby ultimately bamboozling everyone who sees it all, but I guess you'll need to have a clear mind or a third eye to know that what you see is not what you actually get. Most of them will snap all that nice hotels stuff and cars, post it and comment it with stuff like "LOL, living my best life, queen of her own empire, boss lady winning, boujee lifestyle" and all that crap, and at the moment, you actually think that she must really be a hard worker and has earned all that stuff she's flaunting, when in reality the only work she's actually done is just lay down with some rich dude or rich old man and took a snap of everything she saw that's expensive.

Now here's where the problem begins, some people who view all this, there are those that may find out the truth that it's all a lie, and everything these baddies flex isn't actually theirs and it's all just make pretend, and there are those that don't find out the truth. So how does this impact the viewers' relationships? Well let me ask you something, what do you think will happen once a girl sees a baddie flexing all that expensive style and luxury then compares herself with the relationship she has currently, with a man that doesn't own or provide that kind of stuff she starts to desire to have also? Like I said there are those that find out that what they see is all fake and those that don't find out. The problem comes in both ways, there are girls that find out that these baddies are all prostitutes and others are easily funded by rich sugar daddies or old men or even rich married men, but you know what's weirder? Whether the girls find out or they don't about the truth of this fake social media life, most of them won't care, as long as they see the rich lifestyle, they'll believe that is what they also need to do to get those expensive stuff, and I think you're a witness of this kind of stuff also in our societies today, girls wearing revealing clothes while flexing a rich lifestyle with expensive yachts, cars, mega mansions and all that, when secretly behind closed doors, all these stuff are funded by rich old men, sometimes even already married men who couldn't settle down with their wives. So the answer to the previous question is easy, when a girl gets jealous of the sexy, rich lifestyle she sees on media and sees her life with a man who can't provide that for her, she does what she thinks is necessary, dump her guy and do whatever it takes to also flaunt that kind of lifestyle she sees, or not dump him but start to engage in whatever is necessary to get that stuff. Have you ever seen a guy with a girlfriend, yet mostly during the night, the girl is literally a street selling whore? Now I understand why some girls are termed as "she belongs to the streets", at day she's someone's loved girlfriend, but at night she's a woman of the people.

And all this because of what she saw on social media, if she saw the expensive lifestyle of the baddies and how they first look, like how they dress and how their appearance is like, they will imitate what they see, some girls are honestly well mannered at first thanks to good parenting or even religious assumptions, but later on change just because of what they see on social media, don't get me wrong though, constantly scrolling for almost an entire day will put a question in your mind like "what am I doing with my life, those girls have everything I want, how did they get it, while they're not even older than me, what do I do to get all that I desire". And to every question there's always an answer, and what's the answer to comparing yourself to what you see on social media? Do whatever it takes to get what you want, because if you see someone has what you always desire, you're supposed to learn from them right? This is what even our motivational speakers and influencers mostly tell us "get inspired and follow those that already have what you desire or want", except just for one thing, those that actually do have what we want may have not exactly taken the right approach to getting that stuff, so what are we supposed to do, follow them and do everything exactly as they did? That's for you to answer. But it seems this statement has already been embedded into the minds of these girls looking at and following social media baddies. Ending their relationships or even ruining their chances of a proper marriage just because of wanting to live the baddie lifestyle, well you know what they say "if you do the crime, you got to do the time", in this sense, if you want to be a baddie, then you have to deal with what baddies also deal with, and what is it that they deal with exactly? Well, there's disrespect, getting played by men, not getting married, emotional drainage and a lot more. Look, some women may say or think there's nothing wrong with being a baddie for those who aren't baddies already or those who are already one may say being a baddie is an absolute good thing, but is it really though? I don't know what the so called baddies feel when walking down the streets with their fellow baddie crew of five even to ten or more, dressed promiscuously, people staring at them with the eyes of lust and mind of having a one night stand with them or even in a disrespecting gaze, knowing in their minds they literally have to put their bodies at risk to get all the fancy, sexy and luxury.

Sadly, I know some who once were good girls turned baddies, very self-respecting and outward respectable, proper morals and all that, but thanks to social media influence and influence from baddie peers, they are now fully registered baddies being called all kinds of dirty names. Heck, I even know some girls who live a baddie lifestyle but still complain why no proper man approaches them or wants to marry them, and all they complain about is "I'm a beauty why is no man coming up to me, men these days are so weak, they don't even know how to approach a pretty piece like me, men these days only want sex, all the men I've ever dated only wanted to have sex", I honestly don't think any respectable man would want to be seen dating or marrying a so called baddie, and the complaints of not getting a man while they easily have all the answers, just look at the cloth they're wearing the makeup they're putting on, the manners and attitudes they have and all that stuff is enough to make you realize what's the problem.

In life you always get what you put out, when you work hard, you get success well earned, when you work out consistently, you get the body you well deserved, when you constantly crave sex, you'll get the person who even craves it more than you to the point of making you sick, when you are promiscuous, you get a well-earned horny induced man who'll approach you for what you're letting be seen out, so complaining won't really get you your answers. I think we've seen here just how social media baddies are an influence to the fall or breaking of relationships and marriages, it truly is disappointing to see good men being left even at the point when they were just about to marry the girl, suddenly the girl turns baddie and dumps him with the crazy assumption that he can't handle a baddie or manage all her baddie expenses anymore and spoil her chances for a proper future from there on. Honestly speaking, I wish there was something to do to keep modern day girls' minds away from being misled by the social media baddies trend that keeps on growing and growing giving a much darker influence on the young generation and spoiling them just to make them desire a luxurious and expensive lifestyle at the expense of ruining their chances of a happy relationship and marriages.

Now on to the second subculture known as the 304s, these aren't so much different from the baddies except the fact that 304s are already termed as sex workers, OnlyFans girls, or girls that have had sex with multiple partners. In a simpler term, girls with a high body count while living a proud promiscuous life, these are what 304s are, and it's obvious we can see a lot of them, on the streets, places where we live, at the clubs, and everywhere else, and just as the baddies before, we can find these 304s even advertising themselves on social media like twitter or even Instagram, some of them are even pornographic actresses, you may have or may have not run across a post or tweet from a girl commenting something like "subscribe to my OnlyFans, sending my dirty videos for free to whoever likes or follows me, who wants to see me being naughty in bed, go and watch my videos" and more stuff like that, and there are actually men that do all that, pay for a one night stand with her or just to date her or whatever it is they want to do as long as they've paid for her. I can honestly say that I feel pretty disgusted by this, are there even respectable men that decide to start a serious relationship or even consider marrying these types of girls? Maybe there are such men, I don't know, but the vast majority of men I know won't even dare to look at them with respect. I mean just imagine, you seriously decided to date or even marry a 304, proudly decide to introduce her to your friends and one of your friends pulls you to the side and says something like "I know this chick, I paid for her OnlyFans and pounded her hard, she's the one who did group sex with a bunch of men at the same time" or asks "isn't she the girl at a particular adult site or has she stopped doing OnlyFans, she was really good getting railed at that job", upon hearing this, how would you as a man feel? For one thing I can be sure of is that your pride will all fade away immediately that's for sure.

When comparing 304s to body count, I think it's pretty clear here how this is, and the fact that no man wants a girl with a much higher body count than usual, maybe the simps we discussed earlier, maybe, but still, the same way these 304s influence girls is exactly like the same way baddies influence girls, I mean just look at how some or even most of the OnlyFans girls are like, they're literally proud of what they do, even in their profile they advertise themselves as a top certain percent of OnlyFans models, I actually don't know how the statistics works on OnlyFans so I can't really give you a clear stat, but from the way they advertise it it's clear that they see what they're doing is getting them on top and more viewers means more paying, I mean seriously there are a lot of OnlyFans models who can even afford expensive, luxurious cars from what they're doing and they seem really proud and happy of it, are they though? Are women really proud of getting railed at by different men and uploading their videos and selling them just to make money? We all know it's clear that one video sold won't just stick to the one who bought it, you may sell it to two or even three people, but as soon as you go outside it's like the whole neighborhood has bought it, you'll get that "isn't she the chick from that video?" stare from every corner. But it doesn't matter as long as she gets the money, it's no problem to her, she keeps on doing it and ranks up more body count, and more body count means more views, more views means more payments and subscriptions, and soon enough this leads to more influence to more girls seeing this to start also engaging in such activities. Look, times have hit hard, a girl may say she's not a sex worker today, but tomorrow, it's a whole different story, just by seeing a 304 on social media living the good life either as a porn actress or sex worker or 304 or OnlyFans model, the money, the cars they buy, the houses they live in, it's an influence enough to make a good girl go bad. And the problem about this is that all these 304s all seem happy and display pride, I don't think I've ever seen a 304 expressing she's miserable doing OnlyFans or sex working, except maybe retired ones. But the level of happiness they show is enough to tell the viewers that no matter what they do, it's ok, the important thing is the money. Upon seeing this most girls will decide to engage in whatever they see and go do it, and as soon as they see the success, the influence goes on and on and on to more girls to join in the club.

But sooner or later the truth starts to hit hard, most retired 304s, either OnlyFans models or sex workers now have to pay for their actions and decisions. There are a lot of interviews with retired sex workers literally crying in tears that no man looks at them in a respectable way everywhere they go, every corner they go to it's the same "shame on you, you're a filthy whore, dirty and nasty woman" look from people, they even complain that because of what they did, no man even wants to approach them anymore, whether it's at the gym, in a bar or club or wherever it is, even if they are the ones who try to do the approaching, they still get turned down, the very reason which is that she is a 304, active or retired, there even OnlyFans models who cry and complain "my boyfriend left me after realizing that I do OnlyFans" even the ones who were supposed to get married soon "my fiancé called off the wedding after finding out about my past and that I was sex worker", these are tragic results that come after the decisions you make and the actions that follow, a great man once said "Our Lives are the Sum of Our Choices", and since you made the choice to live like that, now you have to deal with the consequences that come with that kind of life. So we can clearly see just how the 304s life have a significant negative impact on women in their relationships and marriages, even as you scroll through social media like YouTube, you'll see a lot of videos concerning 304s, its either 304s just acting out in their regular seemingly called hoe phase or videos of retired 304s complaining that men no longer want to approach them and they're struggling with being single despite the fun had and money made from all the OnlyFans subscriptions and sex work done, because in all fairness, no man wants a woman whose privates and exclusive videos have been seen globally, this is where the MGTOW movement applies to men, rather than deciding to date 304s, they'd rather stick being single and going their own way.

Now we jump to another subculture raised from social media called Sigma males, this tribe is notoriously becoming famous and has a significant impact on men, rather than a positive or negative impact, I would rather say weird impact on men, because there are those who are sigma males and those who think they are or who want to become sigma males. Before I go any further, first thing you should know is that there are different types of males as you've already seen or heard even on social media or from books or something else, there's the alpha male, the sigma male, the beta male of which these are the most common types of males mostly discussed on social media, there's the gamma male, the omega male and the delta male, and each one of them has their own unique traits and behaviors, it just so happens that some are well known and are even more attractive than the other, for instance the alpha male; we all know he's a natural leader, brave, driven by his goals and ambitions, doesn't tolerate bad stuff like disrespect or drama or any other thing compared to the other types of male. But now we're going to discuss this one type of male, the sigma male, there are a lot of videos surrounding this type of male on the internet, whether it be YouTube, TikTok, or Instagram, even funny memes about this type of male. I'm pretty sure you've seen a lot of videos about people explaining "how to become a sigma male, follow these tips to become a sigma male" even videos titled "why women are attracted to sigma males, how to get a girl by becoming a sigma male", so the question comes, why do people want to become sigma males? Can you turn yourself into a sigma male? If you're a certain type of male, is it possible to change into another type of male? And if so it's possible, then why sigma male? Why not the complete alpha male or something else? And can you really handle those traits and attitudes of the sigma male for the rest of your life?

Well let's digest each question one at a time. Like I said and as we all know, each type of these males have their own unique traits and attitudes that make them distinguishable from one another, the sigma male particularly is known in a much better term as the "lone wolf", this is the title most referred to a sigma male, because they are known as the ones who don't try to impress anyone or try to be part of the social class, they have their own beliefs and therefore follow their own paths and norms, being alone never bothers them, you'll find them sitting alone somewhere or walking alone and they never even for once feel the sense of loneliness because they know they have more important things they have to do in their lives rather than dragging along with them baggage of peers or friends. They mostly reject traditional social hierarchies and value their independence and self-reliance. Though there is the assumption that they share charismatic traits with alpha males, but they mostly operate outside conventional norms.

 So why do people want to become a sigma male? Well in my opinion there are two answers for this, revolving around two kinds of people, there are those that want to become sigma male to attract women without all the alpha male principles, and those that want to become sigma male because of what they've been through and now want to live the lone wolf style. Like I said, sigma males may share some charismatic traits with alpha males, like being confident, avoid unnecessary drama and doesn't tolerate disrespect, the major difference is that sigma males are like the 'no caring' type, they have their own lifestyle and don't try to impress anyone and mostly are self-reliant and work alone, they don't need to lead or need to worry whether people like them or not, and they certainly don't need to feel like they can take command of anything or anyone because they know they have it their own way. Now because of some few familiar traits to the alpha male, sigma males tend to attract attention even without wanting to, attention from women or other people in general, because in all honesty, sometimes women are attracted to the type of guy they see as interesting, even though he doesn't display any leadership ethics, just by being not caring and being self-reliant and self-sufficient, in these modern times I'm pretty sure you've heard a lot of women say they like bad boys, well what's one of the traits of a bad boy if I may ask you? Confidence and not caring about anything or anyone, even though they're not in a leadership position. So technically speaking, sigma males are assumed as bad boys to women sometimes, just because of their traits and attitudes henceforth they become attracted to the sigma male.

So now we've got people who want to become sigma males just because they have the lone wolf style and still attract women, I'd say most of these men who want to become sigma males don't exactly possess the leadership charisma, because let's be honest, I don't think leaders are easily made, they're mostly born and we can tell just by looking at how they guide and interact, now upon seeing that being an alpha male requires being a leader, enthusiastic with people, commanding respect, and all that stuff, and since most people can't exactly inhibit all those traits, the best option is to go for the sigma male, because he doesn't need to be a leader, doesn't need to command respect, doesn't need to show enthusiasm to anyone or anything, yet he still grabs attention of women and other people, they even get opportunities that they weren't even thinking of, it's like they have a certain kind of charm or hypnotic effect without even trying, so basically that's why most people tend to go for the sigma male, because this also suits the introverts, I don't think you can easily get an introvert to become an alpha male, that would require talking, interacting and more, but for introverts it seems easy to become the sigma, they just need to be themselves, have confidence in themselves and not care about anything or anyone and everything will go accordingly, will it though?

Like I said before, each type of these males have their own traits, you have your own traits and there's no denying it, if you've naturally got the sigma traits, then there's no denying that you're a sigma male, but trying to turn your traits the other way around to become a sigma is something that is undeniably difficult, let's say you're an extrovert and you're a beta male, this is the type of male that are more agreeable and cooperative and they crave forming relationships, I honestly don't think you can easily change from that to becoming a lone wolf who doesn't need to communicate with anyone or do things their own way, because you're used to who you are and there's no denying, even though you try to change it, even people will be wondering what's going on with you, because you'll be displaying characters that are somewhat seemingly weird to others who are already used to you being who you are and doing what you do.

By trying to change all that, it's going to have some major impacts in your life, it's different from the guy who's been doing it all his entire life already, people will know that he's the kind of guy who just likes minding his own business and nothing else, but if you want to change and force yourself to become someone that you're not, you may copy it but paste it in a completely different manner, for instance; the sigma male is known to be self-reliant and mind their own business, you'll just get the assumption that being a sigma male means ignoring people and avoiding them and completely not giving a damn about anything, now the downside of this is that if you're already used to by people as the guy who talks to people and treats women maybe in a certain way, then all of a sudden you try the sigma way, people are going to start thinking now you're just full of yourself and arrogant, by trying to be attractive, lone wolf, you'll just be seen as the arrogant, selfish guy who's now acting weird, even people will start to avoid you, hence there forth backfires the plan of becoming attractive and getting attention. Look, there are characters and behaviors that you can change like quitting smoking, being a people pleaser, becoming smart, from being lazy to being a consistent hard worker, but traits like being a loner, not wanting to be the leader, not communicating with a lot of people, that's truly something else, you can't just change who you are in the hopes of getting something, if you're extroverted, talk to everyone socially active or a social butterfly, then it's who you are and you have to accept it.

Then there's the second kind of people, the ones who have been damaged and hurt either by love or even just friends. There's a saying that "Behind every lonely and antisocial man is a boy who was betrayed and hurt so much", I believe the saying that "those who are always silent or those who laugh a lot are seriously hurting on the inside". The other kind people who want to become sigma males are the ones who are just tired of being hurt either by women in relationships or just in general. And as a result they tend to find other ways to cover up the pain, some people turn completely cold others try to find other coping mechanisms, the ones who decide to become sigma males view this type of male as the one who is unbothered, because in all honesty how could anyone who doesn't tolerate drama, disrespect or tolerate anyone for that matter go through much pain. Just look at how sigma males live, they mind their own business, self-reliant and self-independent, not even gives you the slightest chance to enter their lives or space, how could you possibly hurt, distract or disrupt this person? It's not easy because their minds are focused on their own lives.

So becoming a sigma male is now considered as a coping mechanism for people, it's understandable because after being through relationships with women who have hurt, betrayed or used you, so it's well known that someone will find some way to cover up the pain, even just being betrayed or hurt or backstabbed by friends is enough to make one go cold. The downside of this though is that upon deciding to go sigma mode, due to the pain mixed with the desire of being a lone wolf, instead of being self-reliant and minding one's own business, the person will unknowingly turn into a self-reliant, arrogant guy, because what you'll honestly be doing is just using copied traits that are not really yours to try to become something you're not just to hide the pain and not have to deal with anyone. In all honesty I can say that this is a plan well backfired in a large percent chance, some may be able to adapt to those traits but a lot of people honestly just go extremely cold to the extent instead of being attractive to people, people even may start being scared of them, but I guess it's what they want and I don't think it's easy to talk them out of it, because once a good heart has gone cold, it's not easy to thaw it out. So the answer to, can you turn into a sigma male and if you're a certain type of male, can you turn into a sigma male, is yes, it's possible, but you'll just be altering these traits without knowing it because of your own nature, if you're a beta male or extrovert and decide to go sigma, you'll just become insecure, and if you're hurting inside and decide to go sigma, you'll just push everyone away, even the ones that have good intentions and are not bad at all. I know going sigma mode may be the answer to what you're looking for, but that isn't the case. For those that want the benefits of being a sigma male like getting attraction and attention from maybe women, there are other things to try instead of living someone else's lifestyle, like trying out what people call nowadays as "becoming the best version of yourself", I won't go much deep into this aspect because I believe you've seen a lot of this stuff on the internet of people teaching men how to become the best version of themselves like reading more books, proper dressing style, talk less and slowly, neat and smartness are key points, build good body physique, build confidence, nofap and all that crap, and I've actually seen this stuff work, people become more attractive and get the attention they want. And for those trying to cover up pain by trying to become a sigma male, there are honestly other ways to get rid of it than going ghost hard cold mode on everyone and everything, I mean there's so much to do, if you want to cry, then let all the pain out on your own time, there's no point in holding it up, you'll just keep ranking it up, let it all out, do your hobbies, do what makes you happy, whatever it is like gym, swimming, making money, anything that makes you happy, learn how to read and understand people, because pain is also our greatest teacher, and because of it, you now know how people are like.

So if you want to become a sigma male, that's fine and nobody's going to talk you out of it, but good luck with handling all those traits and trying not to become something else that receives negative criticisms for the rest of your life, but in my opinion there are literally hundreds of other options to do to get what you want.

Now let's move on to the other type of male culture mostly discussed just like the sigma male, the alpha male, the one we all know or heard of as the bold leader, the confident man, the one who upon entering a room changes the atmosphere with his charisma and presence. Unlike the sigma male who we have seen before that prefers solitude and operates outside social hierarchy, the alpha male is seen as a leader who commands respect and often has a high social status. I'm also sure that you've seen a lot of videos on the internet about the alpha male, "how to become an alpha male, how alpha males choose their woman, why women are attracted to the alpha male, rules and tips for the alpha male", and a lot more on this topic. When discussing about the alpha male, there's only one side to it, people who want to become alpha because they want to command respect and authority. There's a reason why alpha males are who they are, basically it's because of their attitudes, characters and how they live. So now, why do people want to become an alpha male? Well, it's basically because of the benefits they see from an alpha male, just look at it, the alpha male is known to get the women even ten or twenty of them at once, he's known for handling business, he commands respect and no one actually dares to disrespect him, he takes risks, shows confidence in every situation, has the strong leadership charisma, and even establishes a strong connection with others. I like to consider the people wanting to become an alpha male as those who want to become a better version of themselves, because just look at it, there are people who were once, scared, timid or shy losers, no offense. But after doing some minor adjustments, have become something that's unbelievable, a strong leader, confident, a hit with the ladies and more. I'm sure you know some people who were once looked down on, but the unfortunate and the unexpected happened and they had a miraculous change. People who used to fap a lot, people who lacked any ambition, people who couldn't get even a single date from women, but after having enough of their timid lifestyle, now decided to change and came across the alpha male guidance, whether on social media or in the books.

So becoming an alpha male is like a change in lifestyle to become the best version of yourself. So the question comes, can anyone become an alpha male? My honest answer to this is, yes and no! Hear me out first, while the alpha male may inhibit traits like assertiveness, confidence and leadership skills, one may think that's all there is to become an alpha male, heck even an introvert can become an alpha male, despite the fact that there's the need for constant communication, introverts, thanks to their good listening skill and decision making, practicing and following the traits of an alpha male may help boost their character into being an alpha male to being confident, decisive and effective leaders without being the most vocal or socially dominant individuals. Have you ever seen someone who doesn't talk that much, yet still people respect him, he knows how to lead when put in the leadership position, people know he's the guy to handle business and rely on him to lead and achieve something, they respect him, sometimes even fear to show him disrespect or unnecessary drama? Well that's a good example.

So by following and practicing the alpha male traits, one may be considered as an alpha male just because of their characters, though, like I said yes and no, being an alpha male is also a perception, someone may naturally possess these qualities but still doesn't consider himself as the alpha male, he may be a good leader, but doesn't want to be a leader and let someone else lead, he can handle his own business well done, when shown disrespect he doesn't tolerate it and you'll know it, the way he walks may seem a normal guy, but in a particular situation shows confidence, assertiveness, traits like that but only when necessary. Sure he may show alpha male qualities, but even others sometimes won't consider him as an alpha, but just a guy who has his own ways, but the alpha male is somewhat indistinguishable, the way he walks, talks, demands, guides, requests, everything. So yes, you can become the complete alpha male by adjusting to all his traits and get what you want, the women or respect or authority, and no not everyone will fit the exact mold of what is traditionally considered an alpha male, because in all honesty we know there are things even though as hard as we try to copy them, there comes a time where you're just having second thoughts and doubts about it. For instance; being a good leader has its perks, you may want to become an alpha male and possess the leadership skills to lead people, but remember, people are different, you may think all you have to do is lead and tell them what to do, but it turns out to be harder than you thought it was going to be, people have their own mentality and ideas and values, and because of this, it may seem hard to actually lead thoroughly, hence people will start seeing you as just an ok leader, asserting dominance and authority is something else too, you have to maintain your composure so no one gets too scared of you to extent of not even wanting to cope with you, and you may try to portray confidence, but sometimes you need to hold that confidence in particular situations, because sometimes too much confidence may give off arrogant perceptions to others.

So generally speaking, becoming an alpha male has its, should I say rules and perceptions, and becoming one may suit some people, but not exactly everyone, you may have the alpha male qualities but not exactly fit the alpha mold, and some may inhibit alpha male traits but don't consider themselves as alpha males. Some people may even want to become alpha males just to be better at their relationships, for instance, there are those who consider themselves being the one controlled by their partner in a relationship or even marriage, therefore decide to try applying the alpha male life in their relationships, let's say someone is tired of his partner complaining and always trying to take charge of their relationship, even outsiders may think that the relationship is led by the woman and not the man, thus the man decides to take back charge of the two of them by applying the alpha male method, sure it works, there are even confessions of men who were once the ones taking charge from their women, but after going alpha mode have regained their respect they deserved once again. So I guess it's a win for this one, though there's a saying that "too much can be harmful", asserting too much dominance and authority even in relationship can have its downs, being too commanding also can have its own pitfalls, some people while trying to apply the alpha male lifestyle in their relationships may get ahead of themselves and over apply all these habits, too much assertiveness, too much dominance, too much commanding to the extent that even their partners don't feel the intimacy anymore, they just feel like it's being with a programmed soldier and not their authoritative, confident boyfriend or husband anymore. So, doing something isn't bad, but just don't overdo it to the extent of appearing heartless and too much of a stoner.

One more question though, are sigma males and alpha males different? Not exactly, though there are quite some distinguishable traits, for one thing, alpha males are socially active, while the sigma male prefers to work alone, the alpha male builds connection with others while the sigma male is self-reliant and self-independent, the alpha male is a leader, while the sigma male operates outside the social hierarchy and doesn't lead nor follow, but they both don't tolerate disrespect, both are confident in any situation, both handle business, just in their own ways, even the sigma male when given the chance to lead will display outstanding leadership qualities, both don't need validation from other people and both are attractive and get attention each in their own way, the alpha male produces qualities and characters to become noticed as strong and authoritative, while the sigma doesn't try to get it yet still gets it just by being the lone wolf. Some even justify that the sigma male is an alpha male who isn't obnoxious and doesn't show it, so these two may be similar, but are different in their own ways.

Now let's jump on to the subculture that also has an influence on relationships these days, the group that helps you identify the negative and positive signs your partner is showing you, so you can know whether to continue with them or as the people today say "abort mission" and avoid them. This group is known as the "Red and Green Flaggers", they may be the coaching experts or just normal people with experience showing you that the person you're trying to pursue has red flags which means they have certain traits or characters which are bad and if you try to start a relationship with this kind of person it will most likely end up bad for you, or green flags which indicates the person you're pursuing has good traits and characters, therefore you may continue engaging with them. It's all over the internet, videos titled "red flags to look out for in a woman, how to spot red flags, or 5 green flags in a woman to look out for, marry someone who has these green flags", and many more like that. I honestly support this stuff because most likely it's true, just look at it, when approaching someone, they say first impression is everything, and if you clearly pay attention to how they talk, the sign language they give, the way they behave and treat others around them, how they live and many more, tells a lot about them and all you need to know about this person you're trying to approach, whether it's a man or a woman, everyone has their own red and green flags, though most of the videos out there are directly aimed at exposing women's red and green flags a lot compared to men, but that doesn't mean men don't also have their own red and green flags. So maybe it is important sometimes to study something like body language and understand the person you're dealing with, though the issue of red and green flags there sometimes can be a little bit of mix up between the people trying to show you the whole concept of red and green flags, but I guess that depends on who's teaching you that stuff, whether it's a professional dating expert or teacher, or just someone speaking from their own experience. Sometimes you may watch a video of someone saying "if a girl makes direct eye contact with you while talking, it means they're interested in you and adore you, but if she looks away, then she's not interested", then you'll come across another video of someone else saying "if a girl makes direct eye contact with you while talking that means she's not interested in you and if she looks away, then she likes you because she feels shy", so sometimes there can be a little bit of mix up, this point falls down to the eye contact as a red or green flag. Look, it's honestly important to observe red and green flags the person is showing you, whether it be a man or woman, just like when you have a friend whom from the beginning you're talking to, there are signs you can notice that he/she is a liar or can be trusted, same applies for relationships and marriages, but there are people who upon falling victims to their feelings, decide to ignore the red flags they're shown from the beginning, and as a result fall victim to a really tragic relationship or marriage. Let me give you an example; you approach a woman whom upon the first conversation talks smack about her previous boyfriends, why would she talk about them like that if it's over? It's either she misses them, or she has a dirty behavior of gossiping dirt on people, or she's trying to cover up the fact that she was the reason for her previous breakups and she wants to play the victim card, but you ignore it and decide to play along and believe that she truly is just a victim of bad relationships from the wrong men, and now you're the superman that's entered her life and will make everything better now. Or, a woman dates a man that has lied and cheated on her more than once, but decides to let it go, thinking that he just slipped and it won't happen again.

The concept of "people change" sure can be applicable in some contexts, but in some, it doesn't mean you have to be that change, remember, people can change from bad to good or sometimes from bad to worse, a drug addict can change to being saved, a thief can change to a good citizen, but sometimes a thief can change to be a murderer too. There are things you have to let go and let them change on their own and at the right time, but if you try to force someone to change and holding on to the sense that you're the one going to make them change, then you might be the one that will experience the pain that comes from their resistance to change according to your will. You have to accept that you're not God who can change that person, or a therapist to try to talk some sense into that person. When talking about red and green flags for both men and women, there are signs that typically relate to the nature of the man or woman, for instance; one of the green flags on a woman talked about on the internet is that she loves kids or babies, well yes, because that's a natural feminine behavior, like I said before, woman are caretakers, or a red flag on woman is that she wants to be her own boss, yes, because it's not in her nature to be the provider, or even a red flag in man that the man wants the relationship to be 50/50, that can't happen, because relationships aren't supposed to be 50/50, a man has his duties and a woman has her duties, or a green flag in man that he talks about planning a future with the woman, yes, because he has a legacy to continue and he is going to be the one providing and protecting for his family.

In fact, when you look at it, most of the red and green flags are typically from men and women's nature, being a man and knowing what to do and not what to do, and being a woman and knowing what to do and what not to do. There are even a lot of books describing and offering insights into what to look for in potential partners, hence the red and green flags in both men and women, some books are, "He's Just Not That into You: The No-Excuses Truth to Understanding Guys" by Greg Behrendt and Liz Tuccillo, and "Attached: The New Science of Adult Attachment and How It Can Help You Find and Keep Love" by Amir Levine and Rachel Heller, and many more other books out there.

So now, let's take a look at some mostly discussed and even some clear red and green flags in both men and women. Let's start with men's red flags first;

* Avoiding commitment: Like I said before, men plan for the future, but if he's reluctant to define the relationship or make long-term plans, then he might not exactly be the one for you.
* Dishonesty: One of the most important thing in a relationship is honesty, but if he's hiding or keeping stuff from her like important information, then you might want to think twice about him. Though it's true that men aren't exactly supposed to tell each and everything to their women, there are somethings a man has to keep to himself, as long as it isn't something that may hinder the relationship and cause a breakup.
* Inconsistency: There's the saying "a man of my word", apart from being a flag, one of the respectable signs of a man is that he lives up to his word or promises, but if he's actions don't match his words or has an unreliable behavior, then that may be a problem.
* Emotional unavailability: There's a time in relationship even when a man has to put his masculinity aside just a little and show some emotional depth in his woman, not being

feminine-like, but if he absolutely doesn't, or shows completely no interest in her feelings, then it may be a red flag.

* Controlling behavior: Back to too much masculinity, a woman has to be lead and guided by her man, true, but being too much of a commando and dominating may indicate that he's got some personal issues inside him.

* Unaccountability: Not being accountable or responsible isn't exactly a sign of a mature man, being responsible and taking account of every bit of his life is a sign of a man that is good, the actions he takes, the words he says and all that, but if he's not taking account or dodging his responsibilities like providing and protecting his partner and family, then that's an actual red flag.

Now let's turn the tables and look at a man's green flags;

* Respect for boundaries: Just as a man has his own boundaries and respect, he also respects her and her boundaries, and knows doing something might hurt her, damage her or even break her heart, so if he has respect for her boundaries, then it's one of the good signs.

* Accountability: If he lives up to his own words and promises and is responsible like a grownup, then he may be for keeps.

* Emotional availability: You know sometimes, even when a woman is completely down on her luck, or completely angry, all she needs sometimes to calm her down is a cuddle and hug, so if he shows emotional interest in her, then he's good to go.

* Clear communication: Opposite to hiding things, communicating helps build a strong standing relationship, if he goes even an entire month without communication, then you're probably wasting your time, but if communicates often, that's a green flag. Though some men today, thanks to certain online dating coaches, think going a long time without communicating is a sure sign to get her hooked on him, that may work for some girls that claim they like bad boys, but to others, it's a major turnoff.

❖ Honesty: Being truthful to her and not hiding things that may jeopardize the relationship is a vital key to maintain a healthy relationship. But again, a man can't tell everything, somethings are better-off left to the man.

❖ Consistent: If he's reliable, and she knows he keeps his word in everything he says and does, she can trust him, even when there comes a point where she asks him to do something and it is understandably out of his control or unable to, it's ok, because she knows he's still reliable and would do it if it was in his capability.

Now that we're done with the men's side of the red and green flags, let's check out the women's side of the flag, like before let's start with the red flags;

❖ Dishonesty: The apple doesn't fall far from the tree, if she's not honest and frequently lies, then that's a clear red flag to take a step back from her, and you know, hiding things in a relationship isn't forever, sooner or later everything will turn-up, whether its cheating, control or manipulation or to hide the shame or guilt of what they've done to their partner.

❖ Inconsistent values: If a woman's values don't align with the man's, then that may be another sign to stay away from her, there are women who honestly say they don't want to ever have kids in their life, now for a man who plans to continue his legacy, this may be a U-turn for him, because if she says stuff like that, you never know, she may even had or will do an abortion incase things don't go according to plan, and it's a clear sign that your values should align to make your relationship firm.

❖ Needy behavior: Sometimes being too much of a needy person can be a turn off, it's cute that sometimes women show an emotional attachment to the man, but if it becomes an obsession, it might take a wrong turn, an obsession turns into insecurity, and insecurity most likely turns into an overly control manner, and no man wants a woman who tells him what to do.

❖ Emotional manipulation: I can say this is mostly common in most girls today, they tend to use manipulation tactics to control the guy, whether its guilt, crying, playing the victim card or the blame game, even though the woman is clearly the cause of the problem, if she tends to use a lot of this to get what she wants or sometimes just for fun, then that is a major red flag.

* Disrespect: There's a saying a that "a man would rather be respected than loved", and it's true, men stay somewhere where there's peace, sure you may say everyone wants respect, but take a look at how things are in relationships today, most modern women would rather stay in a relationship with an abusive, controlling man, just because he's rich, or physically attractive, or has a certain status and get disrespected, but if a man stays with a woman who controls, manipulates and drives him crazy, he'd rather go live in a barn, even if she's the one who's paying all his bills or even if he promised to care and love her, if he's not getting the respect he deserves as a man, then he's out, so yes, disrespect is also another major red flag.

* Poor communication: Sometimes a woman displaying poor communication traits is a red flag, women are natural talkers, there's even a theory that suggests "women talk about 20,000 words per day compared to men who talk about 7000 words per day", so if a woman tells you she's not very talkative, it could just mean not very talkative to you or she's not interested. I mean, women are literally perceived more expressive or communicative, especially in conversations about emotions, relationships and personal experiences, this can be applied even in texting, if she frequently shows poor communication overall, then just take a step back from that red flag.

Now let's see the green side of the flag;

* Honesty: Honestly speaking, one of the things that women value most in relationship, sometimes even more than men, is honesty, they're the ones who always say they want complete honesty in a relationship or marriage, but it just so happens that honesty is one of the things that modern women can't possess, but the one thing they're good at, and honestly deserve a medal for it, is acting, at first the way she talks about honesty and how she's a good girl will make even yourself think that if the relationship ends, it's all your fault, when in reality there's a whole dark story she kept hidden from you, but still

demanded honesty from you, so my friends if you manage to get a girl with complete honesty, be proud to have seen a green flag.

- ❖ Shared values: If a woman's values and even goals align with the man, then it sure is a green flag, if the man wants to start a business, the woman has the same values or will even support him in any way, if the man wants a long lasting marriage with a family, the woman has the same values, if the man has plans for an adventurous relationship, and the woman feels the same vibe, this is a green flag because your values are both aligned, and you'll plan the same dream, I've seen relationships like these turn into happy marriages, and honestly the results are amazing.

- ❖ Emotional support: Back to the nature of a woman as a caretaker, women are considered emotional beings as compared to men who are considered as logical beings, if a woman shows emotional support to the man even when he's at his lowest, it's a green flag, it doesn't necessarily have to be financial support, but if she's there for him in whatever he's facing, whether praying for him, motivating him or anything else she can support him with, then she's for keeps.

- ❖ Respect: One of the most important factors to look at in a woman you plan to have a relationship with or start a family with, she must have respect to the man, it doesn't matter if she's the one handling all his expenses or the all the expenses in the house, the man still deserves his respect as a man in the relationship, even if he isn't the richest person or the most attractive person in the room, he's still a man and needs respect, so if the woman shows respect no matter what, that's a green flag.

- ❖ Good communication: A woman displaying good communication is a good sign, it's even a motivator for the man to continue whether pursuing her or being with her, sure sometimes she may not show you good communication maybe because she's not interested in you and you feel the urge to leave, sure that's understandable, she may just want somebody else, this is one thing that most people sometimes fail to notice, not everybody has to have the same interest in you, you may approach a girl and gives you low communication vibes and you may start to think she's arrogant or even call her bad names, but maybe that's her way of avoiding you, and you may think you have it all, the money, the good looks and stuff like that, but she'll still give you poor communication vibes because she's not interested and be way talkative and interested in someone who others see as a bum. But if you're in relationship with her or even marriage and she starts showing poor communication vibes, then there's something off, but if there's still a good communication, then that's a green flag.

❖ Good health manners: Women are regarded as clean creatures, I'm not saying men are dirty or meant to be dirty, but when regarding women, they're known to be clean and take care of themselves more frequently compared to men, I mean, who does the cleaning in the house, the bathroom, make sure her man is neat and smart, who does the cleaning when going to the man's apartment or house, women are regarded as clean, but if you see a woman who has a poor health manner or poor hygiene, then that's a major turnoff, but if she's clean and does well to maintain her cleanliness, that's a major green flag in terms of health wise. I don't really know what to say about the modern women though, most of them actually, women these days tend to have the habit of using too much makeup, wigs, long nails, makeup, all of that, which raises the question, how do they manage their health with all that stuff? That's why even some men have said women who have a lot of makeup on or put on a lot of fake stuff are actually dirty or some even claim the women they've slept with have a foul odor. Seriously, how do you go to the bathroom with fake nails the size of a vulture? And doesn't that wig nurture lice? So in all honesty, if you get lucky to get a clean and well health managed girl, she's good.

Now those are just some of the red and green flags commonly discussed, and I'm sure there are a lot more than those, like family background, smoking, partying, submissiveness and the most common one of all, body count. Now I want to clearly touch on this point of body count, and it's mostly a red flag often discussed in women rather than men, some people disregard this flag and say "her body count means nothing, that's just her past, she's changed now", well, like I said, sure she may change, but don't make yourself to be the one to make her change, otherwise you might get hurt.

When talking about body count in men and women, the issue here is completely different, there's a reason why it's mostly discussed in women rather than men, there are even women who explain that a major red flag in their fellow women is a high body count. The reason here is because, women are emotional creatures, and are mostly guided by their feelings, that's why when a woman cries, she might say something or do something that she'll regret later wards, and because of these feelings, in the issue of relationships is where all bets are off, have you ever seen a girl in love? She'll behave like a child, the smiling, the attitudes, everything changes, because she's in love, she'll love this man and sleep with him, if something happens and they break up, she'll get someone else and sleep with him too, the cycle repeats itself over and over and over again, and by doing this, somethings inside her changes, her feelings keep going down and down and down, to the point where she won't matter who she sleeps with next, there are some girls nowadays who say that she's not dating a guy, but just sleeps around with him for fun to fulfill her desires, now imagine if that's your girlfriend having a friend for benefit. So, as she keeps on getting in bed with someone new, her feelings change and is left feeling emotionless, if I may say, and this is bad because once a woman has got a taste of sex over and over and over again, her true feelings and emotions of sex drop, and she's left with a horny induced mind to the point where when she gets a new guy and doesn't feel the pleasure she felt with compared to her previous men, she won't enjoy it anymore and eventually cheat with someone else who thinks can satisfy her better than her current man, and you better hope you're not that current man. Seriously, there's a reason even the online dating experts call this as one of the biggest red flags in a woman, sometimes they even call it "a woman with a large number of mileage", and the ones mostly who end up dating these girls are the ones termed as simps, and the sad reality of this is that women who have a higher body count, when they get into a relationship with a guy who is settled and doesn't have that bad boy attitude or that hit it and quit it character, the woman will be the one to cause tension in the relationship, I'm not saying that it's every woman, but a lot of women who have been in rough relationships with their previous boyfriends, once they get a man who isn't like her exes, she's going to cause trouble, that's why people advise young men to marry girls who are virgins, but in our modern world right now, honestly speaking it's like finding a needle in haystack, I'm not saying there aren't any, there are virgins out there, yes, in this messed up world, there are girls who have successfully kept themselves sealed, overcame temptation, overcame influence, overcame peers and stuff like that. Or if finding a virgin is that hard, at least one with very low body count or low mileage as they say nowadays, maybe one or just two past relationships. So, as a girl keeps on getting a taste of different men, if she gets a man who isn't pleasing her, she'll most likely cheat with another dude who's satisfying her or go back to cheating with her previous ex who was better, even though they already broke up months or years back, she'll just want the pleasure of being pleased once again, and the painful part is that all of this ends up hurting the nice guy who thought he had a chance with her, so it's really disappointing. But what about body count in terms of men?

Like I said before, men's body count number actually doesn't matter, and that's not my opinion, just look around, a woman's virginity is what's mostly discussed, I don't think I've ever heard someone say never marry a man with a high body count, and just so you know, the whole body count thing applies to both men and women, I've even heard stories and confessions of men who have slept with up to 70 women, some even up to 106 women, it's really not something to be proud of, because just like to women, even men who have a completely high number of body counts can too experience emotion depravation, upon having sex with multiple women, a man will start seeing every woman that passes their way as someone just to have sex with, they'll think about having sex all the time instead of looking for the right partner to settle down with and plan a proper future together, some men even confessed that they're life is ruined because of sleeping around too much and now the only thing they can think of is sex even when a proper woman approaches them with good intentions, the only thing they have filled in their minds is sex 24/7. So, even though the issue of body count on men isn't exactly well discussed like women's, it doesn't mean that there are no impacts of sleeping around with high number of partners like you're going to be given some kind of award for doing it, but you know, some cultures even consider men who have already done it to be more experienced, but a woman has to maintain her standards and value, even at times of our grandparents and parents mostly, the dowry was only paid to a virgin girl, but a girl who wasn't a virgin was handed out for free to escape embarrassment, that's why it was crucial for a woman to keep herself sealed, but in today's weak and ruined society, finding a virgin is like finding a pirate's treasure and men decide to settle for or even pay for women who already have a high body count and you know what else, in these modern times, a man who has done it multiple times gets even more attention from women, and more attention from women means that more women also want to have a taste of him just because of the stories that some guy does sex a lot, which means he has to be good, I know some people who, three days cannot go by without bringing in his room a new girl to have sex with, and they don't even have to put in that much effort to get them, because their stories are all over the women's ears, so they're attracted and also want to know and see what's all the hype about, so it just takes a few minutes of conversation and invite them in.

So men choose women with a much less body count, or even possibly a virgin, but women don't regard men's body count because a man's so-called virginity doesn't really matter compared to a woman's. And even when you look at it, men don't need to be pleased, sort of, they're the ones who do the pleasing to women, to make her satisfied, I've honestly never heard a man say something like "I cheated on my woman because she never satisfies me in bed, or I'm living this woman because she never pleases me in bed", unless the woman has completely refused to sleep with her man, that's something else though, but apart from that it's men who do the pleasing, so if they're not satisfactory to the woman, she'll eventually fall for someone else who can, that's why maintaining a woman's virginity and keeping her legs closed is important, because once she opens up, the possibility of stopping is near to impossible, I'm not saying it's completely impossible, but it's near to impossible, she'll sleep with one guy, then go to someone else, get pleased multiple times, and the reality is that men are built different, so someone will make her feel good in bed, and the other won't, or not like the last one who pleased her.

But in today's society, it's really difficult for some women to maintain their virginity and remain humble until marriage, even most girls who say today they're waiting till marriage to have sex, have broken that promise they made to themselves and have already done it, and to make it even worse, they've done it with the wrong person who at first she thought maybe he was going to marry her, but then after the one night stand, he disappeared like a magician, apart from that, there's silly influence from friends, "You are the sum of five people you hang around with", there's a reason someone came up with this statement, if you hang around with five friends who aren't virgins, just know there's a 99% chance you're going to be the sixth one, if you hang around with five friends who are filled with red flags, just know you're going to be the sixth one, if you hang around with five friends who have a high body count, the chances are you're going to be the sixth one, I think you get it, there's social media telling you in an indirect way to use your body to get what you want, use your body as a source of income, and all that stuff, even if she does try to keep her virginity, her friends will even disgrace her "come on girl its modern times, you're not getting any younger, who are you saving it for, you're so lame girl, live a little", from there on the rest is history.

So to put this in a summary, red and green flags are real, and they're honestly something important to notice when choosing a partner, don't just let your emotions get in the way and say "it's just a habit, and people change, I can make him/her better", you're honestly just blinded by heart symbols in your eyes for that person, and if you don't want to believe it, then you'll just have to learn the hard way my friend, and don't just observe one flag and make a conclusion, for instance; you can look at a woman and say she has good communication and accept her, while she's really dishonest, or disrespectful, or look at a man and say he's respectful and say he's the one, when really he just wants to play you and use your body, observe every flag in that person, then make a conclusion, if she or he has every red flag, it's best to back off, but if he or she has every green flag, then go ahead, and still be cautious because people nowadays really deserve a medal for acting, so they may be pretend to have almost or all the green flags, but they're just snakes ready to shed their skin, but you know, they can't act forever, so sooner or later they'll eventually show who they really are, so take your time.

Also just be cautious of the person who you want to approach, she could be a baddie, 304, or a sigma impersonator who has a really damaged background, it's best to stay clear of these people for your own sake, they might cause you pain due to their own attitudes, or from their own mental pain and inflict it on you. And for those who have a body count, my advice is still the same, stay clear of people with a high number of body count, particularly women, if you want change to happen to them, just let God do it, but as for you, steer clear and avoid them, you could get seriously heartbroken, or even diagnosed with a serious disease just for trying to ignore the obvious, and for the girls who've lost their virginity and think their hopes of getting a successful relationship or marriage is over, you still have a chance, though there certain things you need to do and not do, if it's a bad peer, cut them off, if it's a bad habit you have, stop or even get some help, maintain your value, become respectable and presentable in all you do and wear, and I don't mean presentable in lustful way, but if you do this, there's large percent you'll get the right guy in your life.

So now let's move on to the next subculture, the online teachers who we learn from and tell us how to approach and maintain our relationships, the dating experts and coaches. There are seriously a lot of these today, podcasts, Instagram, YouTube, TikTok, everywhere you've got a dating expert to teach you the ways of dating and approaching the one you want, it's like people don't know how to approach and date anymore, like I said way earlier, relationships nowadays are completely different from how they were back then with our parents and grandparents, if you say you can't get a dating coach, consultant or teacher these days, I think you'll just be lying or just don't know where to start as the internet is packed full of them, and that's the problem, there's a saying that "Too many cooks spoil the broth", meaning with so many so-called dating coaches, everyone has their own ideas and opinions and experiences, so it can be confusing to the one who listens to all these coaches, if you've got one particular teacher, that's fine, but if you listen to one today, then another tomorrow, then another, eventually you'll get mixed up in those lessons. So what do we have here on the dating coaches? Well, we have dating experts teaching men to have more than one partner, never text too early, make her look like she's not special, don't be boring, make sure to have sex with her, go out more, talk to as many girls as possible, dress and smell in a certain way, body language matters, build confidence and attraction, you need to have hunter eyes, don't be the one to say I love you first, have unforgettable sex with her to make her remember you, when you talk to her, talk in a certain way, walk in a certain way. Ok, seriously all this just to land the one! I have a question though, did our parents and grandparents have dating experts back in their time though? Maybe they did and maybe they didn't, but if they didn't though, how come their relationships and marriages are so successful and lasting compared to ours? The generation that needs to be taught how to approach and to talk to your fellow human being just because they're of the opposite gender.

And let's not forget about what women are taught by their side of the coach, having high standards, understand male behavior, having confidence to outwit a man, identify red flags, manipulation and control, demanding 50/50, handling rejection, handling a breakup, all of that is being fed to people by their online dating coaches. Earlier I explained that most of these so-called dating coaches, aren't really experts at all, they're just people who went through devastating heartbreaks and have decided to avoid the other gender, and instead of going down themselves, they've decided to drag others along with them by filling their heads with ideas particularly aiming to degrade the other gender.

Have you ever heard people online saying "women are evil so stay away from them completely and go cold, men only want sex, so avoid men at all cost or make a man pay for everything but don't give him anything" and more stuff like that, why do you think they teach all that? Because they're the victims of extreme heart brakes, either they ignored red flags or let the pain they endured change them into people they weren't meant to be, because from what I know is that there's two kinds of pain in this world "pain that hurts and pain that alters", and these people are now spreading the lesson that certain people are evil, and it's bad for the people who listen to all this, they allow it to enter their minds and apply it in real life, that's why we have the MGTOW, the fake sigma males, the baddies, the women manipulators, and all those groups, they're the result of too many cooks in one kitchen.

Now let's take a look at their teachings shall we, what the men are being taught and coached on about. First, I have to admit it, some of their teachings are actually quite accurate, but others are just playing, silly, I mean I honestly paid a little attention to these coaches and what's funny is that most of them teach a lifestyle portrayed mostly by characters either from movies or TV shows, I mean seriously, some of them teach men to live like Bruce Wayne, the Batman character, and other famous characters with certain manly roles, so this got me thinking, so what they're teaching men is how to become like a made up character from a movie, and the characters obviously behave in a manlike manner, which means men today don't know how to act and behave like a man until they're redirected to an antagonist in movie, I've literally seen videos titled "how to be like Batman's Bruce Wayne, How to be a man like James Bond, why every guy wants to be like Thomas Shelby", and more, yet still with all these teachings and lifestyle copying, why are rates of relationship breakups and divorce rates going through the roof, I said before "there is no champion of love", I could just say be who you are as a man with manly traits, but then I could get scolded that in these modern times, being who you are won't get you anything, won't get you respect, won't get you attention, won't get you women, and that's reasonable because I see a lot of people today living a life that's completely from a movie script, behaving, walking and talking like an action hero from the 90s era, and for them, it actually works, they're saying they're getting the women, the attention and all that other stuff, but one thing's for sure, you can't act like someone for so long, sooner or later you're bound to break and revert back to who you really are and all the attention and women and other things are going to start slowly distancing, leaving you to wonder "what went wrong?".

Other teachings, on my thoughts, demand physical appearance changes, there are dating coaches who talk changes on a man's physical appearance, from the hair, down right to the legs, like "as a man, you need to get an attractive haircut, you need to have hunter eyes and not prey eyes, you need to trim your beard a little, you should have a masculine jaw, walk with an upright posture, let your arms sway, walk slowly and in a cool pace", this is literally demanding of changing one's own physical structure, I mean seriously "hunter eyes, masculine jaw", this why even some men today, decide to undergo surgery just to change their appearances, apart from that, there're even exercises shown to help change such features, meowing is a common technique taught on the internet nowadays to change a man's jaw into a masculine one, as they call it, or eye exercises to transform a man's eyes from a prey eyes to a hunter's eyes, I'm sure you've happen to come across such videos maybe one or two. I was a little confused at the concept of hunter and prey eyes at first, but then realized that it meant, a man with prey eyes is a man with weak and sorry looking eyes, and hunter eyes are those that look, well, intimidating and mean like, and people actually do this just to get women's attention, I think if we would've put this kind of effort into other important things like studying or exercise or making money, a lot of people would be far by now, but heck, it's all in the name of love, so be it.

Other teachings from these so-called dating experts include, having more than one partner, men today are apparently taught to also have more than one girl, who acts as a backup for the man incase things with the main girl don't go accordingly, so now men are taught to apply the Round Table Theory as well, except for them it's a bit different, if he doesn't get sex from his main girl, he'll get it from his backup, if he doesn't get peace and respect from his main girl, he'll get it from his backup. The reason for this is that men are taught now to have that abundance mindset, you see like I said before, women are in abundance compared to men, there are even men who have married up to 5 wives or even more, and there's still plenty of women to go around, that's why they're told its crucial to have more than one woman. But not all men do or can do this, some fall hard for a girl, to the extent that they don't feel the need to have another one in the back like a spare tire, but the problem here is, falling too hard is like being too nice, and being too nice, like I said earlier "being too nice will get you used", and its well-known that falling too hard for a woman or being too nice to a woman can be dangerous for a man, even our parents and grandparents knew and well understood this theory, if you love a woman, its good, but don't show too much affection to her, because its known that if a woman finds out that you love her more than she loves you, there's a very high chance she might manipulate you, or some say she may get too bored of you being her yes man and sorry man all the time, and the other issue is that, once men fall hard, it's like they become hypnotized and let their feelings lead and control them. So, to cover this up, men are taught to have the abundance mindset, that's why men today, even though they're going out with the most beautiful girl you've ever seen, or the girl of your dreams, yet he'll still act normal around her, like she's the most normal person in the room, and doesn't do as much things to her as you would've done if you were with her, like compliment her all the time, buy her gifts all the time, make her feel like she's the only girl in the world.

I'm not saying that this is a bad teaching, it's actually good, and I think it's good to have that well-groomed composure, just as a precaution to avoid getting hurt, just don't go too overboard and completely neglect her to make her feel like trash, because some girls don't have that whole diva vibe and actually fall for a guy, but if you go way too far and neglect her, I can't really say the results, but this is why sometimes men pass up on good girls, by going way too in over their heads by living a lifestyle taught and they over applied it.

So is having multiple partners at once good? Well, all I can say is, since there are a lot of women out there, and I mean a lot, if the one you're with does you wrong, you can just find another one, because just look at it, if you're having two or even more women at once, I don't think it's going to be easy to tell one of them that there's two of them, her and her backup, you obviously have to hide each of them from the other. And in doing so, you have to find a way to divide yourself and your time for each one of them, your resources also, but if you can handle all this, then God be with you.

One question comes though, what happens if you date two girls at the same time, keep them a secret from each other and they both really fall for you and they expect you to marry or be with one of them and only one of them? They don't want to share you, they don't want to see you having another partner so they give you all the love you need, what will you do then? You may say "I'll just dump one of them and stick with the other and it's done", maybe, but some girls, and like I said girls are led and influenced mostly by their emotions, some don't take lightly to heart brakes, it can have some really devastating outcomes, she may hate every man for the rest of her life, some even end their own lives, and this may be upon you, and remember, there's something called Karma, 'what goes around comes around'. This is why in my opinion, take it or leave it, you can stay with one girl, but if she proves to be too much of a destruction rather than a construction, you've got a good reason to let her go and find another one, so you can still have that abundant mindset and maintain your composure in a relationship. The reason for why most dating coaches teach this is because it's a known fact that women like men with a masculine trait, and what's one of the masculine traits a man is supposed to have, confidence, by having confidence you assure of yourself that a woman won't shake you nor break you, so you can easily maintain your composure, and women admire this trait, because they know, especially in modern times, a man like that is hard to find, a man who is composed, a man who can't easily be broken or shaken, a man who can't be controlled or driven neither by women nor by sex. So if they get a man with this attitude, they become really drawn to him, that's why most dating coaches teach men this style, because it instills a sense of masculine composure and dominance in them.

The other teachings are more directed into the behavioral traits, by this I mean, the dressing style, walking and talking style, perfume usage and stuff like that. So from being dating coaches, some of them turn into personal life advisors, what a man should wear, what kind of perfume he should use to attract attention, how he should walk and talk like, how he should react. You remember the sigma males we discussed about earlier? As we said, they operate outside social hierarchy, meaning they don't have to follow or adhere to anyone's guidance or teachings, they just do what they do, and still they get women and attention. So, does doing all this stuff work to attract women your way? Well some claim that it does work, others don't really want to do any of this stuff, I mean just look at it, people already have enough in their lives trying to make good impressions whether it's to get a job, start a business, build connections and more, and now they've got to change their lifestyle just to get a woman, it's no wonder men these days no longer want to date or marry, because the dating window just took a whole lot different structure, its more complicated than ever for some reason. So the people who do all this stuff and say that it actually works have to keep up with this kind of lifestyle, I guess sooner rather than later it becomes a daily habit of your life. Dating coaches today teach everything from what to wear depending on a certain occasion, whether you're going out on a date or just going out and you should wear certain cloths to get girls' attention, to the walking style, they teach you how to walk like the alpha male, don't walk dorky or like you lack any confidence, walk in a cool manner so people get your attention and you seem both cool and confident.

There's one other thing that dating coaches teach men today, and to me, this is one of the most accurate teachings I've heard, "don't take women seriously". This is something I have honestly witnessed and did my findings on in today's relationship world, you've heard most women say something like "I want a guy who's sensitive, a guy who can take care of me, love me, I want him to be just the way he is, I don't care if he's not rich or the most attractive, I don't want him to be a bad boy, love is all that matters, I want a guy with a dad bod, I want an emotional man", all this statements and more, yet still they tend to cheat on this kind of guy with the complete opposite of him, they get a rich guy, but cheat on the middle class guy, they get a guy who loves them, cares and has time for them, but cheat on the guy or even fight for the guy who doesn't give a damn about her, they get a guy with a dad bod but get attracted and cheat on the jacked guy. I've witnessed this a lot in today's relationships, women get the guy they claimed they wanted, but cheated with the guy they claimed they didn't want, that's why even men today say they don't know what women want, whatever they say they want, they run towards the complete opposite of what they said, that's why a lot of men today are getting heart brakes, because they thought they had a chance of getting the girl they liked because they heard or even overheard her saying she wants a certain kind of guy, a loving, caring, kind guy, who doesn't demand for sex, gives her gifts occasionally, doesn't have to be incredibly rich, and upon hearing this, they decided to shoot their shot and do everything they heard, be kind, loving, not wanting sex consistently, buying her gifts, and more, yet get seriously broken after finding out that she cheated on him with a guy who has neither done any of that nor like anything she wanted in a man, the bad boy, and she's the one who gives him constant sex, all kinds of it, and the guy who did everything right sits to himself asking what he did wrong. What did he miss? He thought he was everything she ever wanted, and that's where the online dating coaches come in, they teach men today to do the exact opposite of what a woman is saying, whether it's a relationship or a marriage, if she tells you she wants a nice guy, be the opposite, if she says she wants a guy with a dad bod, go to the gym and get jacked, if she says she wants your constant attention, don't give her attention or don't make her your priority, and for some, doing the opposite actually works, relationships aren't what they used to be anymore.

A lot of men today claim women only want money and that's it, partially it's true, money is something most modern women want, but it's only just one of the things they want, men think that making a lot of money will get the girl they want, they may, but then get cheated on by an average Joe, then hear other stuff like, women today want someone who is good at sex and pleases them, the next step is to douse themselves in sex enhancement pills, in my opinion, all these things that women today want, they're natural traits of a man, being physically jacked, that's what men are supposed to be, hit the gym or working out is supposed to be a normal man's routine, be rich, men are supposed to hustle to make ends meet and achieve financial freedom, being attractive, a man making a woman his priority in my defense, is one of the biggest mistakes he could ever do, why do you think most dating coaches say to never make her your priority, because as a man, you have much more important things in your life going on, being a man is already a ticket to going into battle, remember you have to provide, protect, give value and more, so a man's head is supposed to be focused on things that are supposed to make him better, there's God to also be your priority in terms of spiritually, and I honestly don't think a man can focus on this stuff when he's mind is constantly directed towards women and sex, there's a saying in today's world that goes "A man can lose a lot of money trying to chase women, but can never lose women chasing money", that's just a statement emphasizing that men are supposed to focus on their goals and building themselves up whether spiritually, mentally, financially, physically, all that. But if you decide to take the option of listening to women saying they want a certain kind of guy and you change yourself according to her wants and desires instead of your own betterment, then you'll lose every time to the man who knows what he's value as a man is.

Now let's flip the coin and see what women are taught by their dating coaches, here, most teachings are honestly, a bit on the wrong turn if I may say so, some few are on the good side, but it seems that today's modern world, women are fed the wrong ideas. For one thing, they're taught manipulation, you've probably heard of the manipulation techniques women use on men to get what they want, attention, money, things, whatever, and this strategy is taught by these online dating coaches, they teach women how to manipulate a man and how to get what they want, and sadly most men fall victims to these techniques, one of the techniques mostly used is famously known as, the blame game or the victim card, where the woman plays the role of the one who is hurt and affected, have you ever seen a relationship where the woman is the one who made the mistake or did wrong, yet the man is the one apologizing? Sometimes the issue done is quite big, like cheating yet the man is the one who ends up asking for forgiveness, why is that? Because of the blame game.

Online dating coaches that teach women how to manipulate men instill the perception into the minds of young women that one way to get into a man's mind is to make him feel guilty and lose his confidence, that's why when couples argue about something like a woman cheated in the relationship, you'll hear something from the woman like "I cheated because you don't love me anymore, I sacrifice so much for you but you never have time for me, you always work all the time, I gave up everything for you but you never show me love, I have needs too but you never satisfy me" and more stuff like that, and without a reasonable thought in his mind, the poor man falls victim to this game and starts saying things like "you're right honey, I'm sorry, this is all my fault, I'll try to do better, it won't happen again I'm sorry", he's literally apologizing like he's the one who did the mistake.

You know I've seen a lot of jokes on the internet concerning a man who wants to enter into a relationship or marriage, the first thing he should know to do is to apologize without any reason, at first I just thought they were bad jokes, but after careful research, understanding and experience, I now know the rules of the game clearly, and many men fall prey to these games, it's like they're mesmerized and don't even get a minute to think if all this is accurate, all of a sudden they're on their knees begging for forgiveness for the crime they didn't commit. Another well taught manipulation techniques include crying, women sure are led by their feelings, and being led by emotions means it's easy to cry a lot, but sometimes those tears can be crocodile tears, there's something a man does that's truly reasonable that it's his fault, whether he hurt her, disrespected her, broke her heart, stuff like that, that's a reasonable claim to cry, but if she starts crying just because of something that actually sounds silly, and those words are accompanied by words that degrade the man, just know that she either wants something or just trying to get in your head and hide whatever sinister plot she's planning and wants to make sure she gets away with it while the man's blinded by her tears, after all the water works and complaining, the man will feel obligated to do anything and say something like "I'm sorry for everything, what can I do to make everything better, I'll do anything just to make you happy again", if the man really did something wrong to her then this situation may be accurate, but if he did nothing or did something that even may be reasonable to understand and starts to talk like that, just know he's dancing right in the palm of her hands. These are the most common manipulation techniques taught to young women by the online dating teachers, and as you can see, they're mostly aimed at the psychological state of the man, like I said, a man is guided by mind and a woman is guided by emotions, so the way to get to a man's mind is by playing with his conscious.

Another famous teaching in today's world that women are taught by their online coaches is that, a man must be able to provide something, to some extent this is true, the man is the provider of the family, so he must be able and have the ability to provide for it, it's his responsibility as a man, but it just seems that this kind of teaching has taken it to a new level, for instance; women today, as I have said before have some crazy standards that they want in a man, mix that up with the teachings that they have to get a man that has to provide something and you get a woman with an unreasonable number of standards and expectations, its ok to want a man that can provide for you, put a roof over you and the children, food to feed and protection, stuff like that, but today, women don't just want a man who can provide shelter and food, they want a man that can, buy her an expensive luxurious car, plan an enormous wedding, buy her expensive gifts, open for her a huge business, find her a nice place to work like a company, spoil her with huge amounts of money, take care of all her wants and desires, give her things she can showoff to her friends, stuff like that, this is what online teaching from so called "experts" has done to women today, they expect a man to give her all this so as to be called a real man, if he can't offer these, then he should just stand aside, ok fine, you want a man that can provide all this, but the question comes, what will you provide for him? I can honestly say that, a lot of women today demand for so much, yet have little to almost nothing to provide back to the man, you can't just take and take and take and expect not to give anything, when I say provide for him, I don't necessarily mean give him money or buy expensive gifts for him, if you can, that's fine, but the best thing to provide for a man is support and peace of mind, that means support him emotionally, care for him, love him, give him sex, he brings the food home, you give him the meal, care for his family, support him spiritually, pray for him, sometimes men are overwhelmed by the duties of a being a man and don't even have the strength to pray, so it's your duty to pray for him and lift him up, not just demanding gifts and checking his phone, when he's feeling down motivate him to do better, don't degrade him and make him feel more worthless, bring peace to his house and mind. That's what I meant by providing for him. But women today can't even do that, the issue of being taught that a man has to provide something has instilled the notion that men have to prove themselves worthy to get a woman, which means more spending, more expenses, more adventure, and there're men who actually try to keep up by doing all this stuff, but when they eventually run out of things to give, they'll be surprised at what they'll hear, "I can't date a broke guy, what will you give me if you can't even provide for my wants and desires, I need a real man that can handle all my expenses" and more words to make the man feel as if he's failed to accomplish an important mission, that's why some men today now have their own standards, they don't want a woman that doesn't have a decent job or at least a business to also provide money and share the expenses, even though it's not a woman's role to provide. Lots of women today have been rejected or avoided by men under the reason that she has no job or any running business to support her, because as it is well known that since women today claim they want a man that can provide all that crazy stuff, it seems only fair that a woman also has her own means of income to maintain the expenses, you can see here, one thing brings rise to another and another, leading to a world filled with insane relationships. So to the ladies, those dating coaches that teach you to demand men that can provide crazy, unreasonable, expensive stuff, I would suggest you avoid them, because now you also have to show you can give something back out of the nature of your own femininity. There are women who provide the important things of support and peace of mind to their men and get bought everything that you've desired without even them asking for it, it pays to be in your lane and express normal feminine traits.

The next lesson on dating 101 is the usual, having a backup plan. Referring back to the Round Table Theory, we've seen above how women today want a man that's got it all, the money, the looks, the attraction and attention, the sex strength and more, and since its very well known that in order to have all this in one man, you have to create one for yourself, but for those who've managed to get one with all that, then God be with you, but for those still demanding and yet not getting what they want, then why not have one for each desire, a man for the expenses, a man for the looks, a man for finding her a job or opening her a business, a man to cover all her bills and wants, a man that's good in bed, a man that gets attention from other girls, this is another way to cover all her desires and wants. Women today are taught that having one man is not enough, so they need a backup, and a backup for the backup, all in her hand, and each doing a particular role for her. Why do you think most women today can breakup with a man right now, but then after maybe two or three days or even just the next day, you'll see her with a new man? How did she get seduced and accepted him so fast, she didn't, she always had him on standby, if you couldn't cover her bills, he can and is, if you couldn't satisfy her in bed, he can, if you couldn't buy her that new Range Rover, he did, that's the power of a backup, most women today don't feel the emotional baggage that comes with a breakup, because they know there's always someone they've got on standby, incase whatsoever she's not satisfied with the current one, then maybe she'll do with the other one. Heck, she'll even get married and yet still have a backup for anything, that's the power of a well listened online dating teacher, this has become a normal practice today, and men have realized it also, that's why today it's hard to go through your woman's phone or texts or sit next to her without being suspicious, because there's always something to hide, whether a man is paying the bills, or taking her out on expensive take outs, in her mind is "you do your part, and the others will do their parts", every man has his time and share of the words "I love you", because you have to make it convincing that he's the only man, right? This practice is so common now, that even men are doing it, they also have their own backups, in case his girl doesn't support him or bring him peace or just isn't giving him sex, then he has another that'll do all that for him, like I said, one thing leads to another. But it's too late now, these teachings have spread out and all over, women are practicing them with the mindset if no one man can provide, then have as many as possible for each role, that's why some women today, it doesn't take much to seduce her, if she sees you with money, a car or house or whatever, you're accepted, you'll probably think you're loved, but in reality you're just another backup to breakout in case of emergency.

Promiscuity. The purpose of a teaching is to apply what you've learnt in a particular field, and that goes the same with the issue of promiscuity being another lesson taught to young women in this generation by online dating teachers, and we can see every day and everywhere just how they're applying what they've learnt in real life, and instead of a particular field, it's everywhere, on the streets, at the club or bar, in a hotel or restaurants, apartments where people live, it's everywhere, and I mean everywhere, there's no hiding it anymore. In today's modern world, they call it 'sexual liberation', or expressing one's sexual freedom, no matter the number of men a woman can sleep with, it doesn't matter, one of the purpose of teaching promiscuity to young women today is that eventually they'll find the right man, though I don't quite understand how sleeping with everyman you come in contact with will help you find the right man, it just means that you're cheap and nothing more. Not to sound rude here, but the cheapest products in a store are the ones people can acquire easily and more often for their own use, so women today are misled into thinking that promiscuity is one of the ways to get a good man, it's a known truth in today's modern society that men love sex, though women love it more, but it's more widely discussed by men than women that's why there's the assumption that men love it more, it's just that women are shy to talk about it that's why, but anyways, so the thought that came along here is that, since men talk more about sex than women, and men are more turned on easily by what they see in a woman, the best way to get to a man's heart is through sex, right? Wrong, that just means you come at a cheap value, why do you think many women today sleep around a lot, yet don't get married, they eventually get married after being played for so long, after having intimacy with 5, 7 or 10, or even 20 men in her life, they get married at a point where all their feelings are already messed up, sometimes it's just sad seeing women like this. Promiscuity is never a good thing, and it is not a way to get a good man, there are a lot of women out there who thought promiscuity will get them the man they wanted, but now are just being called all kind of dirty names "whore, slut, 304, sex worker", when her actual intentions weren't like that at all.

No thanks to promiscuity, we now have women who are damaged, used, emotionally drained, and some have even decided to turn it into a real sex working job, after sleeping around so much and piling up body counts and yet still unsuccessful to find the perfect mate, the only solution now is to go full prostitute and let it be known that she's a business girl now. Promiscuity is misleading a lot of young women today into thinking that they deserve the right to be free sexually, hence sexual liberation, sleeping around is ok, having multiple partners is ok, losing your virginity at an early age like 12, 13 or 14 is ok, no this is not ok, its driving women into a pit of sexual ignorance, back then our parents and grandparents used to marry women who were virgins, women with the lowest to zero body count and were successfully married, and are the parents we see today, but now, our sons and daughters are having trouble marrying or even keeping a firm relationship, because promiscuity has lied to women that being sexually free is a right, and upon hearing that, most men don't even want to marry such women, some men are turned off just by the sight that a woman is not a virgin, in today's modern times, if a man says he's going to marry a woman with the least number of body count or completely zero, they might want to think again, I'm not saying the stock of virgin women has completely run out, but it's like finding a drop in the ocean. So honestly promiscuity is a total bad thing, there's literally no good that comes out of it.

Finally, there's the good old lesson of 50/50, this is also one of the most dangerous things taught today to women and yet has serious negative complications. Women today are urging on the issue of 50/50, they want every responsibility of a man to be given to a woman also, like I said, if the man is to provide, so does the woman, if the man is to protect, so should the woman. Women have been taught that they've been left out for so long and they've being oppressed to stay inside for so long, but now it's time for them to speak up and stand up for themselves, women are advocating for 50/50 in relationship today, that's why we'll find women campaigning for government jobs, military positions, tough engineering jobs and more. Now, you may say what's wrong with this, they just want to provide a means of helping around with the family or relationship expenses, right? First thing you should know, the honest and hard truth is that women can't lead themselves, a woman needs a man to lead and guide her, without a man, women make the worst decisions, that at the moment don't seem to have any negative impacts, but sooner or later, she'll find out. Once a woman gets higher education, a high paying salary, a good decent job and more stuff like that, she's either going to think that she can take care of things on her own, that's one, the other, she's going to want a man who's better than her and way better than her current man, way better.

Have you ever seen women who are truly successful, and yet are alone, unmarried or a single mother? Why do you think that is? It's because she either thought that she can handle everything on her won or ended a relationship because the man she was with now didn't seem good enough for her, I've even seen this to college students, whom have been paid their college fees by their uneducated boyfriends, but after finishing their studies, are now looking for men who have higher education status, or women who had no job, but after finding a decent job that's similar to her man or even better than her man's, had decided to end the relationship believing they can now take care of themselves or decided that they now want a better man than the one they're with. Women can't lead themselves, they make bad decisions, that's why you can even see most women in modern times who have a high age limit like 45, 50 or even 70s, are going out with literal teenagers aged 22, 24, 28, why? Because of their ignorance and weird expectations, the fact that they wanted a better man and couldn't get one, now their age has seriously climbed, or for those who wanted a better man but failed to get or cope with one, both of these are left single, unmarried and single mothers, yet may be successful, but now hunting young men, the correct term for these women is called "sugar mummies", teenagers today are driving nice cars, staying in a sweet apartment, yet you don't see them going to work, you wonder how they're doing it? The answer is, they have a sponsor, a middle aged woman who made a bad decision in her early ages just because she let success hit her head and thought she wanted someone better or thought she could handle herself, there's a lot of these women out here, and all this started out by demanding a simple 50/50, doesn't seem like such a cool trend now, does it?

And apart from that, if you're demanding 50/50, what are you showing to your sons and daughters? That they should also do the same you've done? Children imitate what their parents are doing and saying and living, the life you live will most likely be the life they'll live as well, and try to picture this for a second, if a woman is taught to demand 50/50, that means both parents need to go to work, who's left looking after the children? The babysitter, boarding school, nursery school? Can you trust these people to give the same parental teachings as the real parents? As I'm writing this, the number of children being kidnapped, molested, or killed is unbelievable, all thanks to women who demanded 50/50 and justified that if the man of the house can go to work, then so should the woman too. Now tell me, do you think 50/50 is still reasonable and worth demanding?

So ladies and gentlemen, this is what's being taught to men and women today, and I think we can both see that what's being taught from their online dating coaches is what's being applied in our modern society today, some are accurate, some are just false teachings, be careful who you listen to and what you put in your mind.

So, to sum it up, today, dating coaches are a lot on the internet, and if you listen to all of them, you might get a little confused and even overwhelmed by all the lifestyle changes they're feeding you, but if you have a particular mentor or relationship expert guiding you through and everything is going good, then proceed as planned, or if you don't have to listen to these online dating "professionals" and the life you live on your own terms gets you what you want, then continue with that, we're not all born with natural charisma, some are, and just by being themselves they get all the attention you could ever want without even them wanting it, so if you want a change of lifestyle to get the attention of a person you like, sure it's not a bad thing, but just be careful to who you listen to in guiding you to change your lifestyle, because some people tend to apply all these teachings expecting it to get them what they want, when in reality, instead of making them more attractive, it just makes them more weirder and more of a repellent rather than an attraction.

Now let's jump on to the next social media subculture we see today, primarily in our gyms, this is one of the weirdest subculture that's risen today, known as the thirst trap gym girls, the name itself elaborates a little just what we're dealing with here. This is specifically a group of girls who are seen engaging in gyms, physically for the workout, but socially for attention seeking, most women these days are put under this term because of what they do at the gyms they go to, one may think they're going to work out, maybe cardio, train their glutes, partially it is correct, but the most reason these girls go there is to seek attention from men, specifically men that they may be interested in. It's well known that women like attention, and it seems that they've figured out that seeking attention on the streets isn't enough, now they go somewhere where there's a collection of men, the gym, don't get me wrong, some do go to actually workout, but the rest are just there for attention, and attention is like air to a balloon, it gives them their pride and the notion that they're beautiful and attractive, other girls aren't even gym material, instead they're just content creators who go to the gym to capture attention from men and post those content on their TikToks or Instagram or whatever, just to feel a sense of pride. And its honestly been quite a complication for men, most men have decided to leave the gym, order equipment, and just workout from home, rather than go to the gym and be seeing or labelled as a creep for staring at a girl at the gym. The problem with these girls is that, since the streets aren't enough to dress promiscuously and grab men's attention, they're now doing it at the gym, the content creators particularly these days, dress in promiscuous manner, they call it "workout cloths", but really it's just cloths that reveal a large part of their bodies to get attention from men, they setup cameras, phones recording and all that stuff just to be seeing as an attractive girl who's getting attention from men even at a gym, the weirdest part of this is that, if it does happen that a guy approaches the woman, the woman will start complaining as if the man is stalking or even harassing her, just so people seeing the video will feel pity, empathy and even demand so-called justice for her, which means more attention from people, the gym and the media as well.

This is insane, you're trying to grab men's attention at a gym, but once a man does approach you, you label him as a creep for stalking you, harassing you or even interfering in your workout session, that's both weird and ridiculous, there's literally no shame these days, some gyms are even facing financial difficulties because a large number of their customers, men that is, are walking out of the gym complaining how could they allow such content and actions to be legal in a gym, some men refer to gym as a place to get their mental and emotional state in order, but if you're going there to tease him and then label him as a creep and a stalker, he's going to get the assumption that women are attention seeking freaks, seriously that kind of attention grabbing is on another whole stupid level.

The term "thirst trap" implies as attention seeking, exactly what they're doing at the gym, grabbing men's attention, although I wouldn't exactly say it's the kind of good attention, I mean these girls in order to grab more attention, they wear promiscuous and provocative clothes to get men to look their way, but when a man approaches them, now he's seen as the creep and the weirdo, and this is clearly another reason as to why men won't approach women anymore today, they see women as people who'll do anything just to get other people's attention, so they're concerned if they do all that crazy stuff just for attention, then what's the guarantee she won't do it again when they're in a relationship or marriage just to get other men's attention? There are a lot of videos on the internet showing how thirst trap gym girls are ruining men's workouts and how a lot of men are complaining that gyms need to put a stop to those who are doing this stuff just to create content for their social media, on the flip side though, online businesses that sell home workout equipment are doing pretty well thanks to these girls who are embarrassing men and cutting into their workout sessions.

Last but not least on our subculture groups, we have the masculine women and feminine men. By the looks of it, as I said earlier during the online dating coaches, it seems men today don't know how to be men anymore, and I think you can clearly see this stuff going around these days, there are men who have feminine traits, on the internet famously known as the "femboys" and now we have women with masculine traits, particularly known as the "tomboys". Women today are becoming more masculine even compared to some men, I'm concerned if it's the drastic decline in testosterone hormones in men or the change in lifestyle, men today are told by these so-called femboys that its ok for men to show their emotional side, they're taught that its ok not to be masculine, and I'm seriously scared to see just how the influence is spreading these days, men are becoming weak, lazy, sluggish, lack of ambition, having no clear goals, submissive, in short, men are becoming like women, I don't mean that in a disrespectful way, but having goals and ambitions is commonly a man thing, women are married by a man who has these things, and men do the marrying, there's a difference, but today, we now have women who are taught to be goal focused and oriented, they're taught to be dominant and self-dependent, they're taught to be the head of the family, and it's also working, that's why most women today refuse to bow down to their men and argue they want the same kind of respect from men.

I don't want to be biased here, but I honestly want to blame the men for this, there's a saying that "hard times create strong men, strong men create good times, good times create weak men, and weak men create hard times", we've had the share of hard times like war and stuff like that which created strong men, and thanks to those men, we also had some good times that came as a reward for winning those hard times, but then we had men that enjoyed those good times to the extent they weren't strong anymore and as a result, they created hard times that we're in now. Modern feminine men have made things a lot harder than they used to be or are supposed to be, because they've enjoyed a lot of the good times and let it ruined their lives, junk foods, pornography, masturbation, not working out or even going outside, lower testosterone, not doing hard work, addicted to scrolling, listening to emotional songs and watching feminine movies and operas, all this stuff has messed with men's way of living and men have let it get into their heads, parents are so disappointed in their children today, sons are confessing they've found their calling and turning gay, daughters are confessing they've found a girlfriend, everything is really messed up. Women are taught that they're the ones that should be dominant and make men submissive, and it's exactly what they're doing today. Women today are told by their fellow women to get a job or start a business, first, for the reason that men today want a woman who's not sorely dependent on the man, and second because men today have become so lazy and sluggish, I mean seriously, men are looking for sugar mummies to take care of them and their expenses, some are even becoming completely feminine by wearing makeup, wearing skirts and girl cloths. And the women are now doing and claiming to want to do the hard jobs that men were supposed to do, join the military, joining government jobs, engineering and construction jobs, they're even wearing men attire now, baggy clothes, participating in sportsmanship and other more masculine recognizable stuff. That's why its easy today for a woman to easily standup to her husband like his fellow man and even engage in physical fight, because they're now taught that they're supposed to be equal, and why not? Even the men today have been brainwashed to become so weak that it's easy to get into a blood sport with a woman, and sometimes even lose to the woman.

In-between I said something about testosterone, this is the hormone that makes a man, well, a man, just like estrogen is the female hormone that makes women be feminine, testosterone is what makes men masculine, a man without or with very low levels of this starts to suffer from mood swings, reduced libido, loss of muscle mass, infertility, loss of hair, and more. No wonder men today suffer from weird disease at a very early age, their testosterone has dropped to the very minimum, and do you know why? As I said, they enjoyed too much of the good times, junk food and all kinds of fatty foods and chemical drinks from sodas to industrialized milk and processed foods, staying indoors the whole day without getting even 5 minutes of sunlight, not doing any sort of hard work, not even 10 minutes of exercise, why shouldn't their testosterone go low, and women now are doing the exact opposite, they're the ones going to the gym, apart from the thirst trap gym girls, there are girls that literally go to work out and exercise, they do the hard work and go out and hustle, no wonder they're the ones now feeling the sense of dominance and control.

Apart from this we've got men listening to soft songs and watching love operas of which portray the man being submissive to the woman; romantic fantasies, chick flicks, romantic dramas and more, again I don't mean to be biased, but these are the kinds of movies women watch, but today even men watch this, and not only watch, but also stick this in their heads and apply it, believing that they may also end up living the Cinderella fantasies, why would a man listen to a song that has these kind of words in them "I can't live without you, without you there's nothing I can do, I would die if I lose you, you're my everything, without you I am nothing"? And they tend to plant these in their heads, that's why we now have men who upon having a girlfriend sends texts like "you're my everything, don't ever leave me because I'll kill myself", this seriously portrays feminine and weak traits of man, that's why men now are being used, cheated and manipulated easily, because it's all they got stuffed in their minds. And now women are the ones more focused on their careers, their goals and are teaching themselves the art of self-independent and self-sufficient doctrines, that's why women now are the ones texting messages like "I'm busy call me back later, can't talk now I'm at work, don't disturb me now I'm busy handling clients" and even screening their men's calls, now women are the ones hustling to put food on the table, and men are crying out they want a woman with a job, now that you've got one, deal with whatever comes with it, since you've decided not to stay in your man lane, now a woman's going to show you who's in charge.

We've got men on the internet advocating that "its ok that men should be submissive, men are not meant to be dominant, no one's going to care that you exercise, its ok for men to be weak, its ok for men to show their feelings", and all this actually enters into the minds of young men, children today are realizing that they've woken up and found out that they're gay, we're losing a lot of men out there, going completely homosexual in the name that they've "woken up" and found they're true calling, it's really disgusting, what kind of calling is that? Relationships are dying, marriages are broken continuously, all because men are failing to do their part of being a man and are going hard feminine, and women are failing to do their part and are going hard masculine. This is the modern world we live in today, I remember a quote from a movie once that said "Men used to be men, now you millennial motherfuckers are running around thinking about what women think and apologizing and shit, it's embarrassing", and this is all true. We need to ask ourselves, is this really a world we want to live in? A world where our sons are becoming someone's girlfriend, and our daughters are becoming father figures, single mothers and lonely old sugar mummies.

Finally, the bottom of our subculture list is the Digital Dating Subculture. Dating, as the internet and social media describes it, has never been easier, someone can just stay inside the whole day and still get a love partner maybe even faster than the guy who goes out the whole day to physically seduce and talk to people, and it actually works, I like to call this as the introverted way and lazy way of finding love, heck, sure it works for some people, even ends up in marriage for them, mostly I like to think this as the cheat code for the introverts or the shy people, others have the natural sense of shyness in them of going to actually face and talk to people, so this online dating stuff really does them a favor, we've got online hookups and even sex-chatting and more online flirting.

Though not everything is for everybody, some people try this, but it ends in a rather unusual and creepy way, some men claim they thought they were chatting with the hottest woman they've ever seen, but upon meeting up physically, it was really just another man behind a woman's profile, and apart from that some people even flirt with married partners, I mean it, some women who aren't satisfied with their marriages, now have the opportunity to secretly create a dating account online and flirt with more men, same applies for men who aren't satisfied with their women, and decide to find hotter women online, discretely of course, so the next time you're chatting with a woman or man, flirting or even more dirty things, just be careful, it could be someone else's lovely wedded partner. The dating market has changed ever since internet became stronger than ever, at first it was just means of communication, but the brains behind it decided to alter it a bit and now we've got people doing online seduction. I am truly amazed and somehow creeped out by this, again, it does workout for some people, but others are just victims for online bamboozlers, and for some, they've actually decided to make it a source of income for their petty crimes, for instance; you may chat with someone on the instinct of flirting and finding a mate or partner, but then the one you're chatting with asks for you to send money to them as evidence that you really love them, once you do, they suddenly disappear, and if you don't, well, they claim that you're not serious with them and even cut you off, and it's not only women doing it, even men are using a way to get some change into their pockets, some men hide behind profiles of beautiful, young, gorgeous women and use it as a cover up to scam unsuspecting men of money under the claim that they'll use it as a means of transport to come see them, or as a way to prove their love for them, but then after the transaction is made, the man behind the maiden vanishes into the vastness of the internet, leaving the poor victim drained and confused.

Back in the good old days, men actually went out to physically talk to women, physically, there were no online dating, not until the rise of Facebook, snapchat, Instagram and more gave way, there were no such things as introverts and shy guys as men had the level of confidence needed to actually walk up to a girl and talk to her, but I guess those days are gone, now that we have social media and all that online crap, if you can't walk up to a girl and face her head on, you can easily find one on a dating app and hope that all goes well, one question though, if it worked for you, does that mean the generation coming after you, will you also teach them that the only way to get a partner is through online and don't need to actually engage physically or will you let them decide and hope it goes well for them?

But you know, it's actually quite funny sometimes, sitting next to someone or passing by someone flirting and even sexting with someone they've just met online, haven't even met their faces yet, but yet sending each other love and mushy emoji and stickers, but that's modern love for you, they say in these modern times you either adapt or get left out, make your choice, will you go with the flow and get a real life online partner and hope it all goes well? Or will you do the same as your parents and grandparents did, the old fashioned way of getting out there and using your natural charm and beauty and hope you find the right one to follow or follow you? The choice is yours.

So my friends, this is what we're seeing going around in our society today, people are living the digital life, literally, some of it works for some people, but for the others it's not exactly a fairytale adventure, my advice is just be cautious when surfing, scrolling or swiping, because in my opinion, social media is like a double edged sword, you can hurt others, you can hurt yourself, but sometimes it does have its good side, but just don't be overwhelmed by everything you see on those sites, not everything is what it seems to be, just because you see someone else doing something, then you assume if you also do it, you'll get the same results, sure sometimes it works, but sometimes it can have devastating consequences, remember "Just because everyone's doing it doesn't mean it's right, and just because no one's doing it, doesn't mean it's wrong", some people have tried to adapt or cope living the modern digital life, but apart from doing online businesses, the only thing they got was regret and pain, some have even gone suicidal just from social media influence.

Live an honest life, please, most of these successful people you see on social media, whether men or women that are flashing luxurious lifestyle, expensive vacations, expensive cars and opulence are either just crooks, online criminals, even homosexuals, and not every online teacher you see on the internet is cutout to be a mentor, some are just victims of destroyed emotions that want to drag you along the line of anxiety and depression. There is no shortcut or an easy way out to achieving something greater, whether it's a relationship or success, live your life straight and follow your common masculine and feminine instincts. I'll understand today if men search for things like how to be a man or gaining masculine traits or manly seduction or even raising testosterone, rather than searching on how to approach a woman, where to find a sugar mummy or how to become a femboy. And I'll understand if women search things like, traits of a good woman, how to be a submissive woman and good partner, avoiding bad peers and maintaining good feminine standards like virginity, rather than searching for, becoming a baddie, searching for a sugar daddy, how to manipulate and control men and how to become an independent boss lady.

BRINGING TO THE TABLE

In today's modern relationships, one of the most asked questions is "what are you bringing to the table?", by that it means, "if I date you or marry you, what will you give me? Or what will you provide for me?". Since women today have way too much high standards like, a man who's rich and successful, who will provide for her and take care of all her needs, and pay every expense for her, then what will she provide for the man? Same may also be for men, if they want a beautiful, young, attractive woman, with a big butt and a curvy shape, what will he provide for her apart from just wanting sex.

Most people today, particularly men claim that women today have nothing to offer, because they see that majority of women now are just sex-oriented, meaning the only thing they can give the man in exchange for him paying for everything and feeding her, is literally just sex, most women these days, refuse what they're nature intended traits assigned to them, like cooking, cleaning, praying for them, caring for them, most women claim that these are housemaid duties, then if that's the case, then what exactly does the woman do in the house if she doesn't even want to get her man ready for work? And what about the man who says he wants a certain kind of girl, he finally gets one, what does he give back in return? There's a kind of confusion in modern days now, some women assume that as long as the man gets the beautiful woman he wants, then he's obliged to pay for everything in a boyfriend/girlfriend stage, even the expenses that are literally parental based, I mean it, some men today are given the father figure duties, they pay for the woman's school or college fees, pay for her shopping, feed her, take her to places around the world, and a lot more, while they're still at a boyfriend and girlfriend level, and the saddest part for the men that do this is that majority of them get played and betrayed sooner or later, that's why a lot of men complain stuff like "I did everything for, but she still cheated on me, I'm the one that paid for her expenses and she still left me", honestly, men are getting plated with the level of father duties, if he does this in a marriage level its fine, but even though it's a marriage level, there should be something promising to show that she deserved all of that, not just sitting around and giving you sex and assume she's done enough for you and expect you to do everything else for her.

And for the men who want a desirable woman, again, don't place fatherly duties on yourself, you have her and she's yours, that's fine, but by giving something back to her it doesn't mean paying for everything as if you're legally married to her, there are some men who get the woman of their dreams, but yet all they do is play with her, by this I mean all they do is demand constant sex from her, women are emotional creatures, at some point earlier I explained that even a hug and a cuddle can make them feel good. There's something like going out on a date, that's a natural habit in a relationship, but some men today don't even do any of that, all they do is use the woman for her body and their own pleasures and nothing else, and because today we have men who are lazy and lack ambition, there are some who manage to get a woman that has a decent job and still submits to the man, and some even give a large percent of their money to her man as respect that he's the man, but what the man gives back is abuse, disrespect, getting mistreated and played with. Some women today in this dark aged world still have that submissive, loyal, pure love, even those who have certain status, despite the fact that women who have a higher status than men tend to be a problem, but I'm telling you, there are those, even just a few, that still remain submissive and still offer respect to the man. But because of actions like these, that's why there are women who complain "men are dogs, all they want is sex, fear all men, what do men want, you get a woman who treats you right, but still play with her feelings".

The actions of the few can derive a conclusion featuring the majority, what do I mean by this? Women who have encountered men that have only used them for their bodies and nothing else, now claim that all men only want sex and nothing else, and men who have encountered women who just demand good and expensive things, claim that all women only want to get spent on, just because they encountered the few minorities of these people doesn't mean that everyone else on earth is exactly like that, but good luck trying to explain that concept to them, they've already made up in their mind that men want sex and women want money, and since its now very well-known, that's why women are enhancing their bodies to level up their game in the dating pool, and men are going extra miles to get money just to impress and get attention from women, so people are doing all this just to impress the other person, it's really a disappointment. Look, don't ever let anyone convince you that there's no more true love in this world, because there is, "Every cloud has a silver lining", in any unpleasant situation or circumstance there's always something positive or good to be found, there are men and women who thought they've lost love until the right person came into their life at just the right time, and now the rest of their life is history.

But coming back to the fact that bringing something is now seen as a physical aspect, like money, beauty, sex and stuff like that, sometimes it's beyond that, if it's all about money, then why did you pay for everything and she still cheated and left you? And if it's all about sex, then why did you give him every kind of sex, yet he still left you for some other chick? Loyalty, respect, submission, care, support and patience are somethings that are honestly hard to find in this modern world, and these are the foundations that help to build and maintain a strong standing relationship to marriage, if these things don't exist, then that's not love my friends, you're just fooling around, you can give him sex, but if there's no respect, he's gone, you can give her money, but if there's no care or support, then she's gone. But today's kids, as messed up as they are, prefer to stay in a place where there's none of that stuff, as long as they have what they desire, some men now decide to stay somewhere where they're constantly getting disrespected on the account that they've got a beautiful, big butt, curvy woman, it doesn't matter if she disrespects him every day, and some women prefer to stay somewhere where there's no loyalty or there's abuse, as long as there's money, so now people are getting attached to material things instead of pure traditional love.

The statement that "women today have nothing to offer besides their bodies" is seemingly rampant in today's world, as of now, we have two kinds of women, those who sorely rely on men for their needs to be taken care of, and the women who work hard whether having a job or a business and claim that they can handle themselves and men today don't bring anything important in their lives. For the women who primarily depend on the man for all her needs are seen as a burden to men, even on the basis of online dating, some women who have the needy trait of wanting something from men, tend to demand or ask for something from the man, whether its money, or something else. And honestly, I can say that this is relatively burdening, how would you feel if someone just keeps asking and asking you for something like money, but you know that there's nothing meaningful they can give back to you, not even support, most women today take this aspect on the basis that the man is the provider, which means he should pay for everything, pay for her night outs, for her bills, for her expenses, her shopping, her looking pretty and stuff like that, while they just look pretty for them, there's one other thing that some online dating coaches teach men today, never engage with a girl who relies on you for everything, a woman who wants you to pay for everything for her but not give back anything meaningful to you, if she thinks sex is the only important thing she can give you, then you might just be dating a liability. Just look at it, the woman won't cook, won't clean, won't support or motivate you, won't get you ready for work, or won't make you feel relaxed after a hard day of work, won't even pray for you, yet she thinks that just by giving you sex is enough to get you going, what's the point in that, is it's sex, he can just easily get it from a sex worker, and I mean it, today, sex is literally one of the cheapest product we have in our society, you can get it everywhere and anywhere, clubs, bars, streets, order it online, now there are even sex toys, so what makes you think that the sex you're giving him is enough for you to ask for anything? No wonder there are even married men who still have sex with even sex workers, because they're tired of the woman that feeds them constant tiring sex and demanding more expensive things, better to just directly buy it. There's a phrase that goes like "Good deeds are rewarded", this particularly applies to the women who know their duties and responsibilities as a woman to his man, she does the exact opposite of what the other woman won't do, the whole cooking and cleaning stuff, yet she gets rewarded with money, presents and more, and she doesn't even have to ask for it, you can't expect the man to carry his husband duties for you while you don't even want to carry your wife duties, that's why apart from men today avoiding relationships and marriages with the assumption that women bring nothing to the table, they decide to date women who are 'completely local', by that I mean women who aren't completely modernized, because they still have that sense of submission and respect in them, apart from modernized women who feel that they're entitled of privileges, special treatments or benefits, without actually having earned them.

The same logic applies to men who demand a girlfriend or wife to give and have everything they want, and not take care of her, if you want a submissive, loyal, caring, beautiful woman, then it means you're also obliged to take care of her, handle her needs as a woman, love her and respect her, and care for her. How is a woman supposed to thrive in her femininity if she has to carry the weight of the man on her? Men, are you making sure your woman is taken care of spiritually, financially, emotionally? How can you expect to be treated like a king if you starve your woman of her needs and wants? Men today are lust driven to the extent that it seems all they want is sex and want their woman to be loyal and submissive while they have nothing to make sure the woman thrives in the presence of her man, it doesn't have to mean buying her expensive things every day, if you can manage it that's fine, but if you don't, there are a lot of other ways to make sure your woman stays in a place where there is authenticity, despite knowing your financial status is low. There are relationships where a woman is thriving happily with her man despite knowing he's like a nobody to others because of his status, yet he does his best and she loves him all the way, while women in relationship filled with money and nothing of the of the foundations of a strong love, quarrel and argue every day, so men, if you want your woman to handle her business and stay feminine to you, handle yours as well and stay masculine as a man is supposed to be.

So to summarize this aspect, the truth is that if you want something, you have to show your worth for it, if you want a kind, loving man who'll take care of your needs and wants, then you have to prove your worthiness of him, not just take anything you want without even giving the slightest glimpse of support, you want him to be like your husband, then be like his wife. And men who want a beautiful, loyal, submissive, feminine woman, be in your masculine lane and remember that if you do get her, now you have to care for her and make sure her femininity spreads across your kingdom, if you want to be treated like a king, then treat her like a queen. But all in all, this narrows down to the type of person you approach and decide to date or marry.

MODERN MARRIAGES

From relationships, we now move on to the next level, marriages, 'the bonds of matrimony', preferably we're going to look at how modern marriages are declining and diminishing in this modern world full of dating coaches, online hookups, media influence and dating subcultures. And sadly, the way marriages are now, is just like how relationships are nowadays, messed up and insane.

First of all, it's a well-known fact that the type of person you choose to start a relationship with or go into marriage with will most likely determine the kind of life you'll have in your future up to how your kids will turn out like, let's say you take an alcoholic and abusive man, how do you think that marriage is going to be like or how the kids will turn out? Or you pick a sex worker woman to be your lovely wedded wife, what do you think is going to happen to that marriage or the kind of influence it will have on the kids? Choosing the right partner to build your family and raise your kids right Is the most important decision a man or woman will ever make as long as they decide that they want to get married, build a family and raise the kids. But it just so happens that today most people choose a partner on the basis of their desires and lusts above what is necessarily a good partner for you, for instance; who do you think a modern woman is going to choose between a man who's successful, wealthy and attractive, yet harsh and abusive, and a man whose middle class, not that attractive, yet has true love, caring and compassion? Or who do you think a modern man is going to choose between a woman who's got a big butt, big breast (most likely plastic surgery maybe), beautiful, yet modernized by the issue of domination and manipulation, and a woman whose normal, skinny body (original), yet has true love, care and submission? Some may say that they'll take the one that's desirable and has the fulfillments of his/her lusts and change him/her to be the right one for him/her, sure, but that's what also a lot of people tried to convince themselves at first, but now they've either committed suicide, seeking therapy help, broken the marriage without it even reaching 1 year, or are the ones now complaining that no good woman or good man is left that has true and genuine love and care, people change,

I believe that too, but it doesn't mean that you have to be the reason for that change, otherwise you might regret it later on.

But sadly, people today choose a partner who is based on what they want instead of need, at first, the person who has everything you want may actually be appealing and having true love and care, but remember, people can act, nobody wants to make a bad first impression of themselves, take yourself for example, if someone walks up to you, maybe asking for help or something, I honestly don't think you'll act harsh and rude or in a bad manner, and that's how people are, you approach a new woman or man today, most likely they won't show you their true dark side they portray every day, as a result you'll end up thinking "I think I just found the right person for me", and after some few weeks of dating and proving yourself that they're right for you, you decide to take it to the next level, you introduce her/him to your friends and family, everybody seems happy for you, your head fills with happiness and pride, until finally the day comes where you both say "I do", from there on just give it a few more weeks, and it's time for the person you thought was right to finally takeoff their mask and show you just how people deserve a nomination for being the best faker.

The other most important thing when choosing a lifelong partner, is waiting, patience is something a lot of people can't practice in their lives, if you found someone that by your eyes you see they're the perfect partner, just wait a little, don't rush things, get to know them more deeply, their habits, their lifestyle, their background, their family, even the people they surround themselves with, I'm not saying do a complete stalking trial, but studying the person you're with will sure do you some good before making a terrible decision that you'll regret for the rest of your life. Some people take marriages for granted as if it's something normal like eating a cake or going to the bathroom, there's a reason they call it "taking it to the next level", just look at all those people you told about your partner, the struggle and expenses you went through to plan the wedding, your parents, relatives, the fear and anxiety you faced of standing in front thousands of people declaring that someone is your husband or wife, then suddenly after a few months or even a few years, they see you going to court to demand for a divorce and ask you what happened? Your response may probably be like "she/he wasn't what I thought, things didn't work out", and they'll most likely ask you "well didn't you know that, you chose him/her, didn't you know they were like that?".

Back then with our parents and grandparents, they didn't rush things, even though they found a woman who's a virgin or a man who's successful, they had to get to know them better so as not to make the wrong decision, if they had made the wrong decision, don't take this harshly, but mostly likely you wouldn't have been here, and if you don't believe me, one day maybe even sit down with your parents and ask them what it was really like back then finding the right partner, heck funny enough they even hired some close friends to scan the person they wanted to make a mate in their lives, just to get to know them better. But today, we've got men who marry a woman they're attracted to by their eyes, and the harsh truth is that men are attracted to what they see, so if they see a woman with all his wants, desires and lusts, he's unfortunately going to let his lust drive him into making the wrong decision of making her his lifelong partner. And likewise for women today, they're more attracted to the guy who's driving a nice car, wealthy, attractive and sexy, and decide that this is the person to marry who'll take care of all her needs. And I've honestly discovered something that may be the obvious, have you realized that most the people who have the lusts and desires we crave, have the least care and true love, yet those who most likely don't have them, have the most care and love? Just an observation though, and don't take it the wrong way, there are people out there who've got it all, the stuff and the love, and those who don't got the stuff nor the love. So basically we now have people driven by the desires in their minds, for men it's more of a sexual desire, for women it's more of a material desire.

One of the things dating coaches teach today, for men particularly is that, if they want to choose a woman to likely marry, they should use their minds instead of their lusts, most men today are easily driven by sex that's why they make the wrong decisions, there's a song I know titled "Thinking with my dick", and that's what most men today are doing, instead of listening to their brain telling them to carefully study and understand the person they want to approach, they let their desires do the thinking and let their minds regret their decisions later on. And for women, it may be unclear that women are like programmed to find the best man for them, earlier on I said this also applies to the animal kingdom, the better man gets the woman, but today the desires and standards are through the roof, they don't even seem to care that a man is already married or has a woman, they want a piece of him too, just as long as the man has what she wants, they keep feeding themselves the idea that a man who's rich and successful is the ideal guy for them "what's a poor man going to do with me, I don't date broke guys", this is what they're feeding their minds with, and as a result, they choose an abusive, uncaring, unfatherly figure in her life. Sometimes the best advice when choosing partner is to look at your parents, for a man to choose a wife, look at your mother and you'll see what woman you'll most likely be drawn to, and for a woman, look at your father and decide what kind of man you'll be drawn to, this doesn't mean that everyone follows this pattern, and it's not a strict rule, sometimes people may use their conscious as a way to avoid any negative traits they see in their parents and wish to avoid them, so that's just a side advice.

Today, marriages are seriously crumbling and it's all because people made the decision of choosing the wrong partner in their lives, marrying then remarrying again is a common practice today and people don't even feel ashamed anymore, they take the phrase "I want a divorce, let's get a divorce, we're getting a divorce" as lightly as saying "hello world". Marriages today are seen as blessing if it manages to surpass even a year without breaking down, conflicts are a natural state in any relationship or marriage, in fact they're even necessary as some may say, so that people can get to know one another better, and they're actually right, at some point you have to argue about something, whether it's logical or even ridiculous, because through this, then you can really get to know your partner, what they like and don't like, who they really are, and stuff like that, there's no such thing as a perfect marriage, not even our parents or grandparents went through their entire marriages without even disagreeing at some point, sometimes conflict rather than being a demolition hammer, it can be a building block to get your matters in order. Some people even make weird promises that they won't ever argue with their spouse in marriage, and that's being too silly, you argue with your friends, with your parents sometimes, your relatives, you may even argue with yourself at times, what makes you think you won't argue with your wife or husband? There's no such thing as a perfect marriage, no matter how perfect a married couple may look like on the outside, trust me, you don't want to know what they're going through when they're behind closed doors, some couples may tend to compare their relationship with other's and see themselves as arguing a lot and say "I wish we were like that couple, they don't argue, always smiling, always happy, just a big happy family", think again, not all that glitters is gold, the couple that may seem all joy on the outside, may turn out to be the most grotesque when they're alone.

For men, choosing a partner to build a family or spend the rest of your life with is the most important decision a man can make in his life, don't take it as ordering a burger then off you go, the woman you choose today is going to be the mother of your child, your outside identity, the caretaker of your house, the mother who didn't give birth to you, your soulmate, your best friend and even your partner in crime, which means, you have to choose the right one for you, just look at all those titles for one woman, and you're out here choosing a woman just because she has a big backside, fake lips, fake body but nothing in the head, how is she supposed to do all that for you as a husband if she was chosen under the preference of her beauty and looks and not under the preference of a good, submissive, loving woman to enlighten your house? Think carefully before deciding, don't let your erection determine your direction, a lot of men did this and now they're facing the consequences. Between a man who's decided to stay single and a man who's made the worst decision of marrying the wrong woman, I honestly think the man who remained single got the better end of the deal, first of all, the wrong woman in your life will be the influence to your kids, as a man, you're the one who trains and provides for the kids sure, but most of the time the kids are with their mother watching what she does or speak, this is going to have a major mental impact on the kids, some fathers later on see their kids changed for the worst and ask "where did I go wrong", you may not be the cause, but because you chose the wrong woman to look after your kids, now they're messed up. Also, choosing the right woman means choosing the right identity for yourself as a man, in marriage, the woman you choose is your identity to the outside, if you choose a woman who's submissive, loyal humble, loving, respects herself, people are also going to respect you and know that this guy wasn't joking when he was looking for a woman, and the compliments won't just end at your friends, your parents, relatives, even workplace will be proud of you and realize that this guy made the best decision of choosing the right woman, but if you choose a woman inspired by your crazy desires, people are honestly going to be shocked at you just as to how and why would you pick someone like that, they won't blame the woman, they'll blame you, even though the woman is the one with the dirty or nasty traits, still, the man is going to be the one being pointed fingers at, because the woman is a man's identity, that's why it's very crucial that men choose a woman who'll be a wife material, I know there are a lot of women out there who may seem charming because of their beauty and body shapes that may mesmerize you, but you have to look past all that and decide to choose the one that's best for you, your future and your family, its honestly not as easy as it is to say "we're getting a divorce" in front of your kids, your parents, for you it may seem easy just to pronounce it, but how will all those people perceive, and by the looks of it, more divorcing stories and testimonies may just keep filling people's heads with the assumptions that "wow! So many divorces right now, maybe there aren't any more good women out there to marry", your poor choices may serve as a justification for the more coming younger generation to refuse to marry, because so far we already have those kind of people right now, men who have already admitted that they'll never marry in their lifetime, because of the assumptions that no good women are left out there and by seeing the rates of divorces pile up, that may be enough evidence to say that marriages aren't worth it anymore, but can you blame them? They're looking for inspiration that is worth it to marry anymore or are all the women we have on our planet now not worth it anymore? So please men, choose the right partner, you aren't just doing it for you, you're also doing it to inspire the future generations that despite the wicked world we're in right now, there's still hope for a working out marriage because if somebody's marriage is working out then maybe theirs will too.

And as for the women, the same goes too, choosing the perfect man for your life is the best choice a woman can ever make, it's just so sad that today, modern women look at what's on the outside rather than what's on the inside, women today look at what the man drives rather than what drives the man, because of the assumption that successful and attractive men are the solution to fulfilling the woman's needs, now we've got women even arguing for one guy just because they see he's wealthy and attractive, and at first approach, he may seem all that and welcoming and everything you want, but as time goes by, you'll soon come to realize that not everything is what it seems to be, I've witnessed women married to a rich guy, but what they endured in that marriage made them even desire just to be with an average guy, because, even though you don't want to accept it, it's the truth that women are emotional creatures, when you get a man that's got it all, just know the amount of emotional availability for you won't be as you expected it to be. Like I said, women today have crazy standards, a rich man, handsome and attractive, good in bed, high status, in short they put it like (6 figure income, 6 feet tall, 6 pack Chad), all these standards have messed up their minds to the extent that now, most women have a picky habit in men, whatever man comes up to them, they look at his status, appearance, does he look rich? Is he handsome enough? Is he attractive to other girls? What's his financial status? Is he just an employee or a boss? Without regarding that he may be the best option of a great father and husband, instead they choose the ones who seem to have the higher status symbol, but in the end tend to be the one who's the most unfit for the father/husband figure. This may be the reasons as to why in later years, most women complain that they can't get a good husband, these are the women that later on pickup any good guy that come their way after facing a certain number of divorces with men they chose according to their physical desires, and they're also the same women who spend all day at church, crying out to the priests to lay a hand on them as they claim to can't get a good husband or stay in a sustainable marriage, sometimes the reason is just because of your poor decisions that you couldn't accept and are now looking for a way out. As for women, the issue of identity is somewhat different from men, let's say a woman chooses a man who turns out to be a drunkard or an alcoholic, most people won't judge the woman, because its known that men do the marrying and women get married, so the inflicts go to the man, though this doesn't mean that it doesn't affect the woman, it does both emotionally and even mentally, she'll feel pain, embarrassment, regret as to why she even allowed herself to get married to that man in the first place, emotionally uncared for, mentally ill, seriously, some even go for therapy for this, that's all because of the poor choices you make in selecting the suitable mate for your life, just look at how your parents or relatives are going to see you like for having a husband who turned to be not quite as you thought, but for your friends though I wouldn't be too concerned about them, because for some reason, women have a weird jealousy towards each other, they see their fellow woman bought a new car or house or get married, they start getting jealous or even hope that everything you have crumbles down, though I admit it not every woman is like that, but its well-known that majority of women feel a sense of intimidation seeing their fellow women excel at something, now if you've made the wrong decision of choosing the wrong partner for your life and marriage, just know when everything falls down they'll be there saying sorry in their mouths but in their hearts they're saying "finally, you got what you deserve", so why not prove them wrong and choose the best man for you to build a strong family.

When talking about modern marriages there are few things that need to stand out, you might have heard that the generation we're now leaving in is somewhat referred to as the weak generation or the weak society, primarily because of the decisions made by both men and women, but mostly the men, you might have heard of these phrases "weak men, weak society, modern weak men" every once in a while, whether outside or on social media, but I honestly don't think I've ever heard of weak women, why do think it's mostly referring to men? Because men are the ones who built the world, the society, men are the ones who are responsible for everything, even the fact that women today are becoming on top compared to men, or women becoming more hardworking and self-independent or the rise of masculine women and feminine men, that's all for the men to blame, men today are weak, and marriage rates declining is no exception, just look at these statistics;

❖ At first there was the generation of men who married virgin women.
❖ Then came a generation of men who married non-virgin women.

❖ Then came a generation of men who married women who did abortion.

❖ Then came a generation of men who married single mothers.

❖ Finally, a generation of men who married women who were not virgins, who did abortions and were single mothers altogether.

You can see just how our generation has gone down the hill here, women's standards are going up, while men's standards are going down, now men will settle for any woman provided that he can get her to bed and have sex with her. I've seen videos, and maybe you have too of older men, much likely like our grandfathers being disappointed just how men have lost their touch in this modern world, and sadly it's the truth as what we're seeing now.

Thanks to spoiled women and weak men, modern marriages now have men and women who are demanding for 50/50, women want to also be head of the family as the man is, that's why when it's time to go to work, both of them will leave early in the morning, they're both busy, both have business or work assignments, and you might be thinking "wouldn't that be nice so the woman can also be contributing to the family", that's just the thought of a lazy man, again, demanding for 50/50 is not a standard, it's a modern man's way of saying "I'm too tired or lazy of handling all my responsibilities and want a woman to also share some of them", and if it might be true, then why are the number of divorce rates somewhat associated with partners who apply the 50/50 rule? And remember this, if she's at work, how sure are you that someone better than you won't get his way with her? There are a lot of testimonies about this, be careful.

This is just nonsense, back then they never had something like this, but yet their marriages are still thriving, because men were masculine and knew their responsibilities as a man, and women were feminine and knew their duties as a woman, but because of social media, globalization and rapid decline of reasonable men, we now have both genders who want to share roles and duties, that's why even in some marriages now, women are the ones going out to work and put food or something to the table, and men are the ones who are staying inside, cooking, cleaning, looking after the children, the man is the woman of the house and the woman is the man of the house, does that seem like 50/50 to you? To me that's just gender role switching. First of all, you as a man will lose your respect and self-respect, and second, don't be surprised or pissed off to one day you find out that your wife has been cheating on you with a work colleague or boss, all because you wanted a woman who'll also go to work, that's all on you.

Look, marriages are supposed to be led by masculine and feminine instincts, but now they're just led by men who use their emotions and are controlled by lust, and women who are overzealous with standards and guided by social media teachings. And what's funny is that, just to prove the point that men and women back then were much better than now, young girls in today's society are dating married men, as I said, men back then knew where their masculinity stood, so they were in all masculine, crazy enough, even the women today claim that modern men have got nothing on older men who are married, they say they're better in every aspect, masculine frame, not guided by emotions and not easy to control, better financially and even better in sex, as crazy as it seems for them to expose themselves saying all this stuff, but it's the truth, men today are getting disrespected on a whole other level, just imagine it, if a modern day's man marries a woman, suddenly later on he comes to realize that his wife has been cheating with a much older man on the claim that the older man was better in bed, was better financially and wasn't easy to manipulate compared to the modern day husband. And there must be a line of shame drawn somewhere, I mean how could a strong healthy man in his 20s get told that he's nothing compared to a man in his 60s? Because modern men have lost their masculine frame.

My honest advice to men, remember you're the one doing the marrying, don't rush things and eventually regretting it in the future, especially now because women have stepped up their standards level, and as a man you should focus on being the best version of yourself first, sure there might be peers or family persuading you to marry early, marriage isn't something to be talked into, you have to be ready for it, but if you do it under the condition that your friends and family told you to do it, or you're comparing yourself to others that they're getting married so why shouldn't you, or some men think that entering into marriage will fulfil their crazy sexual desires, or you have a woman with all the goodies you crave and decide to wife her, if you do it for any of those reasons, then you're going to find out the hard way why marriage is called the next level.

And for women, again, marriage is something to be taken seriously, don't just jump into it on the account that you've found a rich and attractive guy and you want to secure him as your own so you quickly jump into marriage, a lot of women have tried that but now they're left divorced and not a man approaching them because they were already titled as "somebody's wife" or left as a single mother struggling to look after her children. Be careful and be cautious of the men that approach you or who you find attractive, some are not who they appear to be, its known that marriage to a woman is one of the greatest things that happen to a woman, that's why at the wedding, the woman is the one who's more hyped about it, the man is usually more nervous actually, but to a woman it is something great, that's why your parents are so proud of you, your besties congratulate you so much, some of which are even so jealous of you, because you get titled "somebody's wife", build a family and raise children, a lot of women have been approached by men and fed the lie that "I will marry you", and sadly had fallen prey to these mesmerizing words, but after giving and doing everything for the man, those plans and promises are now a history, you have to be careful in choosing the right man for you, a serious man.

I can't believe out of all those teachings that women dating coaches give to women, the least and I mean the least thing women are taught is how to spot a good man, a serious man to make their boyfriend and husband, most of the teachings to women on how to spot a good man is explained by men, so women need to listen to men's teaching to spot a good, husband material man, or if not to men, listen to women who are now dealing with divorce or left as single mothers, the women that had their fair share of wrong choices in choosing a man, now has common sense in her head and is trying to educate women on how to find a good man. Don't be the kind of woman who teaches other people based on the terrible experience she's had with women, sure you can learn the basis on how to spot a good man, there's red and green flags, instead of listening to women who teach you how to manipulate a man and being promiscuous, you can even listen to men's videos or podcasts as they explain on how to spot a good man, or a husband material man, that's something that may be useful for you.

So that's my take on to modern marriages, and just like modern relationships, they are seriously messed up, that's why men don't want to marry anymore, thinking there are no more good women out there, and some women now don't want to get married and decide to build their own life and call themselves the "boss lady". But all in all, there's something very important on the issue of marriages that may also be a driving factor for men and women to make a bad decision in marrying the wrong partner, let's see what it is shall we.

PRESSURE TO MARRY SOONER

The pressure or influence to marry sooner can lead you down the path to selecting the wrong partner in your life, there's external pressure and internal pressure as well. First of all, the external pressure may be from seeing your friends getting married and also you wanting to have your own marriage, there's influence and push from your friends and family "you're getting older, marry soon, why haven't you marry or gotten married yet, hurry up and marry, I want grandkids", getting pushed by all those influences may drive someone to make a decision they'll regret for the rest of their lives and see marriage as sour as lemons. Apart from that if we take a look at the internal influences we have the age factor, someone may see that they're getting older when in reality they've not even hit the 30th age mark and want to marry as soon as possible in the fear that as you get older no one is going to want you, this is why you shouldn't rush to marriage, you'll end up with some disastrous results.

As the saying goes "don't follow the crowd", this isn't just a term of phrase, there's a reason why they came up with this statement, if you do something just because you listened to some people, the results may not be pleasant for you, you can listen to advice about starting a business or investing or becoming better in every aspect of your life, but listening to the advice that you need to marry fast is something else, why do you think even the online dating coaches rarely advice on marriage or marrying early? Because this is a whole different level from just dating. Some people get into early marriage because they want to fulfil their bodily desires, like I said, men's minds today are filled with so much sex desire that some assume if they get into marriage just to have all the sex they want it will calm or cure them of their lust, sadly this isn't true, you'll get into that marriage and still cheat outside for sex with other women, other people marry after seeing all their friends around them marrying and starting a family, being happy on the outside that they finally have a wife or husband, now it's making other people jealous and also want to marry quickly, but this is wrong, just because you see other people around you marrying doesn't mean that you should run head first into marriage, to get into a marriage you have to be ready, it doesn't mean being ready in terms of age wise, which brings me to the issue of age in terms of age factor. First of all, don't let anyone tell you that the appropriate age to marry is 30s or 40s, being in a marriage is your readiness mentally, financially, emotionally and psychologically, a man can have all these by the age of 25, are you going to tell him to wait until he's 30 or 40 to get into a marriage? Is he mature mentally? Yes, is he financially stable? Yes, is he emotionally capable? Yes, is he spiritually stable? Yes, then what's stopping him to marry?

Going into marriage means that as a man you're mature enough and know the responsibilities of a man to his wife, family and his own as a man to provide, protect and care for the family, and for the woman to get into a marriage means that she's ready for the duties of a wife, mother and caretaker of the family and house. Here's hint; age factor doesn't matter, if you think that someone will be ready for marriage in his/her 30s or 40s then think again, there are men who are 30s but are like teenagers, meaning they're not mature enough to handle adult responsibilities, they still want to play around with women, get drunk, get wasted, got to clubs, do teenager stuff and all that, do you think this guy is ready for marriage? And there're men who are like 24 or 27 but are like in their 30s, they're responsible enough and know their duties just like a full grown man, they know how to handle their finances well, they know how to handle a family well, are you going to tell him to wait for his 30s to finally bring a woman into his life? And likewise there're women in their 20s but already have the wife/mother charisma, they already know how to handle a man and children as if she's already been into different marriages, she's submissive, loyal and respectable to a man, is she supposed to wait any longer? Or women who are in their 30s but still want to get laid, go to clubs, hangout with their friends, fool around with men, seek constant attention from other men, are you sure she's ready for a marriage? There're people who may look young but have the mentality of a full grownup that know their responsibilities, and there're grownups but aren't ready for the adult lifestyle, so marriage really isn't about the age factor, it's all about readiness.

Apart from that, in the issue of age factor, earlier I discussed something about men and women's value and how women's value doesn't stay up for so long while men's value stays up for long, most women intend to get into marriage as soon as possible because they're well aware that their value won't stay fresh for so long, some women who are at the age of 20s, especially mid 20s like 25, 26, 27, society expects them to get married at that age, even their parents at that age ask them whether they're going to get married or why aren't they married yet? Because their value won't stay for so long as soon as they hit the 30s age mark their fresh charisma of being called a beauty starts to fade away, most likely in today's society they're referred to as 'aunties', because it's considered that their age for being a sweet chick has reached its peak, and this is one of the most reasons why some women whose age has gone later on start to accept any man that comes their way as long as they love her, because they feel left out and because that no one wants to approach them anymore. But just look at it, sure society expects women to get married at the mid-20s, but are these women actually ready for the marriage, or is it just a force expectation, especially in this era where most women at that age feel like it's time to spread their legs and fly, I didn't mean wings, I actually meant legs, just look at what women at that age mark are doing, going to clubs, getting drunk, promiscuity, smoking, losing their virginity because they think it's now cool to do that, racking up body counts, now tell me, do you think this kind of woman is ready for a serious marriage? Shameful enough I've even heard testimonies of women who are already in marriage at the 20s age mark but are complaining that they don't feel the freedom they deserve, they claim they still want to go to clubs, drink, hangout with friends and more of that hooligan stuff, now I don't know if they were forced into marriage or they just got married because they feared their value would continue decreasing, this is why it's very crucial for a woman to maintain her virtue, because if she doesn't then her later years won't be so pleasant to her. Here's an interesting theory regarding women and their age factor in relation to marriage;

- ❖ When a woman is under 25, the chances of getting married are over 75%.
- ❖ When a woman is between 26 and 29, the chances of getting married are 50%.
- ❖ When a woman is above 30, the chances of getting married are under 25%.

I don't make the rules, that's just how nature planned things, but this doesn't necessarily mean that women above 30 will never get married, no, but it all depends on the issue of maintaining her virtue and her readiness of becoming a wife and mother, some women may say they're ready to become a mother sure, but what about being a wife, this is the part that women mistakenly mess up, especially most women in this era, the issue of submitting to a man, getting denied the privilege of going out to drink and party and hanging out with friends until its late night, if a woman wants all this yet plans to get married early, then she might want to sit down and re-plan that whole marriage thing because otherwise she'll just mess up the man's life and cause him unwanted tension. For a woman, being in a marriage means being able to submit to her man, showing obedience, love, support, care, loyalty, but if you can't provide any of this, then just get yourself in order first, and it doesn't matter whether you see your friends around you getting married and you want it to happen too, prepare yourself first then the right marriage will come to you, is it better to run into marriage just because of your neediness or because of your friends around you, only to destroy it and end up in pain and humility? Or is it better to maintain your virtue and value and wait for the right man to come to build a strong standing marriage and family? You decide.

As for the men though, again, in my opinion age factor isn't exactly a primary factor, rather maturity and the ability to handle responsibility is, but if we take a look at the facts, the age limit for a man to enter marriage is above 30s, why? Because a man in his 30s and above seems to be the man that has built himself financially, mentally, emotionally, meaning he is considered as a grownup or adult, so he can marry now at this age, here's the men's age factor in relation to marrying;

- ❖ When a man is under 25, the chances of getting married are under 25%.
- ❖ When a man is between 26 and 29, the chances of getting married are 50%.
- ❖ When a man is above 30, the chances of getting married are over 75%.

So we see here that men's age limit is preferably from 30 and above, the few percent that are below that may consist of the men that are already mature enough and well-built to handle responsibilities of a husband and father. At the mid-20s, it's the age known by many that it's time for the man to build himself, he may be in college, building a business, investing, learning new skills, getting in shape, making money, building himself mentally, so by the age of 30s he's expected of having achieved if not all this then a large number of it thereby making him eligible for marrying someone's daughter. Some think that being financially stable is the only key to enter into marriage, I know some people, and maybe you've seen some rich people whose marriages have crumbled, what happened? They had the money right? True, but just being financially secure isn't the only key to a successful marriage, it may be the most important, but not the only one, you can be financially secure but not responsible enough to handle children, a father has to be able to lead, protect, train his children or family and build them up to be well raised sons and daughters, otherwise, whatever happens to the family is on the man's hands. Some men were financially secure and ran into marriage thinking all that was needed was money, and what happened is that they kept giving money to their children, and giving and giving, to the point they became spoiled brats and messed up, now do you think money is the only leverage for a good marriage?

One of the advices a man is given when choosing a woman to marry is that the woman has to be younger than him, for instance; if the man is maybe 32, the woman has to be about 25 years of age, because the woman still has fresh value, beautiful, still has virtue and maintained her virginity and even if not, then at least she has very low body count, but this is the kind of stuff that I wouldn't mostly say about the women in this generation, today a woman whose 20 years of age has already enough body count and has done sex more than the average 50 year old woman, younger women today are more sexually active than our grandmothers ever were, that's why it's becoming more of a challenge for men to find the right woman to marry, because they're filled with promiscuity and naughtiness, there are men who force a marriage with a modern woman in the hopes that maybe she'll change once getting married, but the results were very unpleasant, some weddings lasted 2 years, some even just a couple of months, this is really messed up, there was even one that lasted 6 hours, unbelievable.

One more thing to note, there's difference between marriage and wedding, most people are excited about the wedding and forget about the marriage duties, and this is especially about modern women, earlier I said that a marriage or wedding to a woman is one of the happiest days of her life, while to a man is somehow a bit paranoid, women are so excited about the wedding all the celebrations, the food, the attention, her family seeing her getting married, that she forgets what comes after just those few hours of celebrations, comes a lifetime of duties, commitment, submission and more, and after finding out about this later, then they start complaining that it's not what they bargained for so start to willingly or unwillingly refusing wife or even mother duties, wedding is just like a graduation where you've finished a certain degree of school or college and now you're going to look for a job or going to a higher school level, or you've celebrated your birthday but what comes next is old age, so don't let all those celebrations get in your head and forget that there's something bigger coming after that, I'm not saying you shouldn't be happy, happiness and celebrating is a must, but just don't be attracted too much to the festival that you forget about your motherly or fatherly duties.

So all in all, marriage is a beautiful thing, but just don't get into it with the expectation of impressing or copying others or just because your parents keep pressuring you to do so, sure maybe they did it early, but there's a difference between our era and theirs, ours is powered by social media, dating coaches and immoral lifestyle, theirs was powered by loyalty, virtue, good character, love, responsibilities and more like that, and back then it was easy to find a man who was responsible and mature enough to handle fatherly and husband duties and responsibilities compared to today's men who need teachers to show them what it means and how to become a man, likewise for women back then were raised in virtue, submission and good moral, but today we've got women who know the taste of sex even better than married women, we now have women who even at the age of 18, 16 or 20s already are not virgins and have 10+ body counts, so in these modern times just be careful who you marry or get married to.

THE RISE OF DIVORCE RATES

When discussing about modern marriages, you honestly can't leave out the issue of divorce and divorce rates, and in all honesty, the divorce rates these days is absolutely insane, and it's just not me saying it, there are actual statistics explaining this, even divorce lawyers are saying something about this. And you may ask, if it's true that divorce rates are high nowadays and still going up, then what's the reason behind these divorces? Why is it that people are breaking up so much and ending their commitments and engagements they promised to their faces in front of everybody?

In a short answer I'll just say it's the result of choosing the wrong partner, but is it really the only reason as to why so many marriages are breaking up these days? Or is there something else to it? Well in an honest opinion, marriages today are, first of all regarded as a business, particularly for some if not most women, second, marriage today is regarded as an escape route either for shame or embarrassment, thirdly, marriages today are assumed to be a way for someone to satisfy their thirst for sex, and forth, marriages today are just not taken seriously as they were back in the old days.

What do I mean when I say regarded as a business for women, whether you're in a marriage or not and may have heard of something called "child support", due to the current economic hardships people are facing, some women have decided to regard marriage as an opportunity for them to prune men of their money, most men's marriages today are not safe because women have made it their mission to enter into a relationship which by all means will try to ensure that they get the man to marry them as soon as possible, then after a while maybe months or a couple of years and after having a few children, they'll finally come up and say that they're tired and want a divorce and will claim full custody of the children and make the ex-husband pay for everything, the prune size depends on your financial status, seriously, if you're incredibly rich, the financial obligation you have to adhere to will be insane, I've seen a lot of successful men, entrepreneurs, athletes, actors, artists, who had their marriages broken by the woman and then demanded an incredibly high amount of child support, I'm sure you may have heard or even seen something like this also, it's not something new anymore, it is a new source of income for modern women today, if she's in desperate need of money or needs to pay her bills, all she has to do is beautify herself, get the manipulation techniques right, lure some rich man, or even if he's not that rich, just some guy who'll fit the demand pattern, start a relationship and make everything seem as if it's going straight for the guy, then start demanding marriage from the man, "babe if you really love me, then why aren't we married yet, time is flying-by, we should be married by now, why haven't you introduced me to your parents yet, don't you love me, I thought you were serious with me, a serious man would've already put a ring on my finger", and because the guy is blinded by the fact that their relationship is going great, he'll have no other choice than to make it official and plan the wedding, once that's all cleared up, the next step for the woman is to find a way out of the marriage and put an end to it, she'll decide to have a few children with the man as an extra income tunnel, then all that's left is to initiate an argument, either frame the husband for something he didn't do, cause unnecessary drama into his life to wear down his mental status, then finally claim a divorce and demand custody of the children, and since it's the law, you can't say no to it, so you have to pay up, and she finally has enough money to cover her bills and then sum.

No wonder even some of the dating coaches today are teaching men not to get married, because they've realized that women today are not looking for love, they're looking for help, that's why they get into marriage, and after a few months, the woman starts behaving in an unexpected way, later on she wants divorce and half of what the man owns. And it's really sad, men who have hustled and struggled to get themselves to where they are, financially and even status wise got it all ruined by a woman who wanted to cover her expenses, leaving the man to crumble down, feel like he has to start over again in his life, this issue is getting men both scared of entering a marriage because of the fear of losing everything they have, and angry at women for realizing that they're now using marriage as a means of generating money, marriage isn't a business, but in today's world, it apparently is.

Here's an interesting theory shared by a divorce lawyer that might shed some light to this point, "Men don't file for divorce or leave a long-term relationship unless they already have someone else lined up. 70% of divorces are initiated by women and they will end a relationship and be alone. Men don't do this", so here you can clearly see that, women are the ones who initiate a divorce much more compared to men, and one of the primary reasons today is to get the man's fortune. Though, there is a technique that men have also started doing nowadays, which is dating for a long time, but no marriage, yes, you can see a couple dating for months and even years, yet they don't tie the knot, why? Typically because the man doesn't want to face the obligation of paying child support to the woman, so instead they just date and date and date until death or breakup, but you will never see a ring on both of their fingers, this tactic is also practiced by celebrities or even some of your friends are doing this, you may see them loving each other as if they're already husband and wife and do everything that a married couple always do, living in the same house, having children, sleeping together, travel together and all that other stuff, yet they're not married, you may wonder "these two have come a long way, why aren't they married yet? I can't believe after all this time those two have been together they're still not married yet! Why don't those two get married, they're already living like a married couple anyways?", you may have all these questions in your head, but the man dating the woman has all the answers he needs as to why he doesn't want to put a ring on it yet. And sure some relationships may go on with this habit for even possibly years, like I said until breakup or death do them apart, some women aren't exactly thrilled with that habit though, either they know because they won't be able to get even a dime of the man's wealth and so just decide to call it quits under the complain that "you don't love me, all this time we've been together and you still haven't married me", though there are women who may not have those intentions in mind and decide to call it quits under the astonishment that everybody knows them as a couple for a very long time, but are wondering why are they not officially married yet, so to avoid the questions and confusion, its best just to end it, or there are women who have an incredible love for their man that they're not troubled with the fact that they're not married, "I love him so much, and whatever he wants to do I won't go against it, I'll agree with everything he wants".

Apart from that, the other reason divorce rates are so up is because marriage is now considered a route to escape shame, like I explained before, women have little time to hold their values, that is at a certain age they are assumed to have been married, which is particularly in their 20s, otherwise, as soon as they hit 30s, society will start marking them as aunties or middle aged women, and because women don't want that to happen and also to impress their family and friends that she's getting married, she'll hurry up into marriage with a guy who she thinks is the right one for him, as a result, after few months into marriage, she starts regretting her decision after seeing the man is abusive, disrespectful, not caring, not providing and more, what's the solution to escape this? Divorce. Some women look around and see all their friends getting married and starting a family, and also decide that they too want a piece of the action, so they run headfirst into marriage without considering what marriage really needs, but she'll find that out on her own. The same goes for men, some men enter into a relationship because of either peer pressure from their friends or family, so he plans everything, the wedding, getting donations from friends and family to build up the wedding, then finally calling it official, but after a few months of seeing the responsibilities as the man of the house, family needs, children needs and wants, work-marriage life balance, wife handling in case he chose the wrong woman, all that starts to seem like a burden to the man and so he has two choices, either call it quits or go on carrying the burden and hope everything will eventually workout, that's why despite all this, men are the least who initiate a divorce, sure they may initiate it out of the reason of the problematic woman, but some choose to carry the weight of the marriage and accept the responsibility of their decisions, so I know it's heartbreaking, but there's a saying "You'll learn the hard way" and this is the hard way, so you'll learn what marriage is really about.

Apart from that, we now have people who are craving or driven by lust to the point they think that getting into marriage will cure them of their insatiable hunger for sex, yes, there are people who go into marriage just for the pleasure of sex, it may sound ridiculous, but one thing I actually couldn't believe is that it works for some couples, though in a modern term this applies to those couples who are regarded as both being "nasty and freaky", similarly to what a marriage requires, two people who share the same energy and vibe, more likely as best friends, even though they might argue once in a while, but hey even twins argue and they look alike, but having someone who you share the same energy, vibe, ideas, opinions and more, is something beautiful actually, and I guess this point applies to the couples who've gotten married under the principal of satisfying their sexual desires, they do all the kinds of sex they could ever dream of and plan of not having children, so they married just for the fun of satisfying themselves, but that doesn't mean that everybody should imitate this, again, your vibes and energy must align, otherwise you'll just seem like a pervert or porn-addicted idiot to your partner, if you ask me in a total of ten couples, one to two couples maximum may get into a marriage to satisfy their sex cravings, and because their energies align together, so if you find a soulmate with the same crazy fantasies, then God be with you, but if you're not that kind of guy or girl and want a more subtle and respectful marriage, I suggest you work on yourself first to attract the right partner to you, just remember the saying "You attract what you are", so if you're a sex-induced person you'll most likely attract a person with the same vibe, and if you want it to be like that, then it's up to you, because some may think of the subtle ones as boring and want a more thrilling and sex-active person but if you're a more subtle and charming person, well just be sure you choose the right one for you, because if you make the wrong move of choosing one with a different energy, like being sex-driven, then the results might be complaining that the only thing your partner has to offer is sex and nothing else important.

So, to put this altogether, marriages today aren't taken seriously as they were back in the old days, people today are marrying just for the sake of being married, either because they want to cure their loneliness, or because everybody else around them is doing it, or because they're being too pressured from their friends and families or because they think they can have all the sex they want, and there are probably a lot more reasons beyond these, reasons of which might be a contributing factor to the rise of divorce rates today. Marriage isn't something to play with, ask yourself this, if your parents or grandparents decided to get married for all the wrong reasons listed, do you think you would be here today? Maybe, but probably a result of an accident while playing around, or may be seen as a burden because they didn't plan for it to happen, not to be disrespectful though, but just take a second to think about that and you may recognize whether marriage is something to play with or realize that it's something to be taken seriously.

Marriage, in an honest opinion is for people who are ready to adhere and accept the responsibilities of a grown up, a father, a husband, a wife, a mother, and member of a new family, either someone's aunt or uncle or father-in-law or mother-in-law, a man who is ready to handle the responsibilities of providing and protecting and a woman who's ready to care and nurture, but if you as a man see yourself as not ready, whether financially or mentally or not responsible enough to handle a family, then I suggest you get yourself together first before you ruin someone else's life or waste their time, don't rush things, if you think that you're not yet financial stable to handle a family, that's understandable, because your goal is to not only be responsible, but also be able to financially secure your family, get your goals first then plan the next step, don't just let random people, either friends or family tell you to rush and get married, unless they'll be helping you to take care of your family, wife and kids, that's another story, but apart from that, it's your decision and goal, so get yourself right first, then decide that you're now ready to marry.

And for the girls, in modern times its honestly difficult but not impossible, there is a benefit of being modest and moral driven, have you ever seen women who, maybe in high school or college were considered as the lame and boring, yet they're the ones getting married earlier more than the ones who were more promiscuous or provocative, that's because a woman's value is in her ability to stay humble, decent and moral, this way it's a more easy way to attract a respectable man to start a relationship and eventually getting into a successful marriage, stop listening to those "dating coaches" or friends who tell you to be something that'll make you regret doing in the future, a lot of women were supposed to get married early with the right man, but because they chose to listen to the wrong friends and do bad things, now they're regretting every step of their actions, and now that they've all grown up, they're the ones filled with cries in churches, on the streets, complaining that they can't get a good man or get married, just stay modest and you'll see for yourself. And the issue of getting into marriage for the sake of gathering the man's wealth, that's honestly not a good idea, first of all, it'll always come back to bite you in one way or another, second, think about the children, you're depriving them of fatherly love and a father figure, this may not be in all instances, but women who tend to raise children on their own, the children may end up being something horrible in the future, daughters raised by single mothers tend to adapt to their mother's behavior and have the mentality and attitude towards men, and sons raised by single mothers may grow up without knowing the true ways of being a man with responsibilities or a father. And apart from all this, there's something called loneliness that you'll come to deal with, women who think they've won by pruning their ex-husbands' money think they've made it in life, but really they're just setting themselves up for being lonely, old women, I know a lot of women who did the same and are now using that money to bribe teenagers to hang around with them or show them affection, just imagine, a woman in her 50s dating a teen in his 20s, just because she's lonely and needs love or just misses the sex adventures, and this is what's happening and going on in today's world. So please women, if you want a marriage, you have to be sure that you're ready to be loyal, submissive, humble and respectful to a man, some women entered into marriages, but after discovering they can't hang out with their friends anymore like they used to, they have to ask for permission from their husbands to go out or do something, they can no longer go clubbing or drinking or do anymore of that nasty stuff, they realized that marriage is like a cage and have been complaining ever since, these are women who were honestly not ready for marriage, so if you're not ready, don't waste somebody else's time and get yourself in order first.

Apart from all this, there people who have decided they don't want marriage at all, I mean they don't want to marry or ever marry in their entire lives completely, sadly I know some people, and maybe you know some as well, I honestly don't think someone is born with the mentality that they never want to marry or get married at all for the rest of their lives, its either something happened that broke their hearts and altered their minds, or they just got brainwashed or something, and they are really emphasizing on this that they will never change their minds on this, well if there's one thing that life can teach you is to never say never, I've realized that most of the people that say that they'll never do something in their entire lives, usually are the ones who become well known for doing it, life has a really weird way of turning things around, even if it's our own decisions, it will make it seem like we have no other option. Anyways, I can't change your mind whether you should marry or not, but please ask yourself this in case you made the decision of never wanting to marry in your entire life, what's the reason for you not wanting to marry completely? Or what was the cause that changed your mind and made you rethink about marrying? And picture yourself 40 or 50 years from now, who do you think will be besides you, caring for you and looking after you?

THE HARSH REALITY

I can confidently say that, in terms of relationships, we have really hit rock bottom, the world is messed up and I wish I could say that everything will be alright soon, but I'll just be lying to myself and be making a false statement, where we are headed, the only way to get things right again is if both men and women stand on their values and morals, but if that doesn't come to pass, then I'm afraid the term 'love' and 'relationships' will be something dreadful, and not just to us, our children, and even grandchildren will be victimized by what we're doing today. I take a look around and feel sad of our generation, and even more sadder when I realize that our next generation is going to be probably even worse than ours, people say that the dating pool today is hard, just how do you think it's going to be in about 5, 7 or even 10 years from now, and the hard truth is that we've all brought this upon ourselves.

I remember someone who said "dating is so hard now, everyone is on guard, a whole competition, who calls first, who is less mushy, act like you don't really need them so they don't get too comfortable, etc. you can't just be yourself anymore, very stressful", and its true though, dating now is more like a game, a business and like a training you have to go through. And to make it worse we've added some updates to make it even more sickening, like I said before, we now have feminine men who are guided by their feelings and driven by sex, the modern terms for these men are; dick-driven, soy boys and the usual term 'simp', these are the kind of men we mostly have today and it is sad, men now are competing, even fighting to get one woman who isn't even interested in both of them, even worse a woman who is substandard, no offense, but that's the truth, back then we had men who would go to war to fight for a good course, to fight for their country and their generations and their legacy, but today we have men fighting each other for a low value woman, and if that's not enough, men fighting for someone's wife, does this seem right at all? No it is not right, apart from this, we now have men filled with pride that they've slept with a lot of women compared to another man, as if there's a competition for ranking up body counts, all this is because men can't control their urges anymore, they're guided by what's between their legs than what's inside their skulls. We've got men who are afraid to go outside and talk to girls, men who pay for

OnlyFans or online flirting with a digital woman, men who stay indoors watching pornography and jerking off to their screens, men who listen to mushy love songs and apply it to women thinking it'll make them look romantic, men who would rather buy prostitutes just for sex and because they don't want to approach women, are these the kind of men who would actually be fit to be strong father figures, strong husbands and good family leaders? Sorry to break it to you, but the answer is NO. And it's no wonder that women have seen the kind of men we now have and decided to increase their standards and expectations, they see men now are easily controllable by big butts, big breasts and pretty faces and have realized that it's easy to manipulate and control them and raise their standards, while men just want a woman who can give him sex. Sadly, this is the generation we're now living in, we now have men who don't have any standards at all, they'll take any woman provided he's able to get sex, while women's standards are going through the roof, just look at the reality, men today aren't even given a chance by women if they don't have enough to bring to the table, that's why there are so many men on the internet motivating men to work hard, the word is cruel now to men who don't have anything to offer, society won't like you, women won't chase you, family won't respect, friends won't follow you, where are you to go and what are you to do? But the honest shame is that men today have no standards at all, they'll settle for anything less, if women have all these standards then why can't men also have their standards?

Listen, if men in the world were to demand something from women, and actually stand on their demands, who do you think in their right minds who deny it? They would be insane to reject those demands, because men are the leaders, providers, builders and protectors of the world, but now men's minds are full of junk and sexualized, they'll let their lust do the thinking for them. This is why most relationships today and marriages are broken at their early stages, because men are choosing women according to the hunger of what's between their legs. We now have songs and movies filled with genres of lust, sex and money, and its what's filling the minds and corrupting the men and women today, just look at it, songs filled with sex and lust contents get men aroused and lead them to do the stupidest things just for sex with a woman, songs filled with money contents depict to women that having a man with money is everything, that's why right now as a man if you don't have money as one of your benefits, no woman will even look at you, what you drive, what you wear and what you own will be the determinants for you to get a woman, if you don't have that, just stand aside.

Apart from this, we see men listening to mushy songs and movies where a man is portrayed as a softy, and by being this he is able to get the woman he wants, but that's in the movies, try and practice that stuff in real life by acting romantic and soft like that, if it worked for you, then you must very proud and I hope your relationship continues to prosper, but for many men out here doing all that junk are seriously getting heartbroken, played and used, it's because men aren't supposed to be like that, being a man means you're supposed to be strong, courageous, bold and confident, let that mushy and soft stuff be for the women, but instead, today we have men texting a woman stuff like this "I can't live without you, please don't go, you're my everything, if you leave I'll die, you're the greatest thing that ever happened to me, without you there's nothing I can do, I am the luckiest man on the earth to have you, I forgive you for cheating just please come back to me, if you ever leave me I'll kill myself", are you sick or something? Worse enough you are sending these texts to modern women, women who are focused on being baddies, 304s, slay queens and gold-diggers, yet regardless of all that, you choose to ignore that and say "I can change her, once we get married I'll make her listen to me and change her ways", good luck with that, just know that many men before you have tried and are now victims of manipulation and strong heart brakes. There's this modern statement that goes like "These days, men put in five times more effort than their grandfathers to get a woman who is fifty times more promiscuous than their grandmothers", seriously, men who spend a lot just to impress a woman, men who even do witchcraft just to seem attractive to a woman, and sometimes not just any woman, but somebody else's wife, men today even have challenges on who will be the first to get a certain woman, just because she's pretty on the outside, has a big backside and curvaceous, without regarding if she has anything important to offer, but no, that's not what men today are looking at, they prefer to look at her physical appearance, and maybe that's why the surgeons' offices is full of women today who want to enhance their body size. It's really sad and degrading.

Apart from that, we have damaged women, let me ask you something, do you know why our ancestors preferred to marry virgins? I mean apart from a submissive, loyal, pretty woman, virginity was the top aspect that they were looking for. Because a woman who's already slept around with a lot of men tends to start determining and comparing the taste and character of each man, I mean look around, I explained earlier, you may say that money is all you need to get a woman, then why are there rich guys out here getting cheated on by their women to a dude who doesn't even give her a dime? She'll say "because his sex game is better", there are even women out here confessing they left their millionaire boyfriends because he couldn't satisfy her in bed to be with someone who's still hustling just because he satisfies her well. There's a secret in being decent and maintaining virginity, but I guess most women today don't recognize that, women who have slept with a lot of men are now termed as 'damaged women', because once she gets a taste of one man, then the second, then the third, then the forth, from there on once you come in, just know she'll be comparing you to her previous men she had intimacy with, and if you're not that great compared to her previous ones, just know it's only a matter of time before you wake up, check your phone and see the "I think we should see other people, I don't think this will work out" text. Now I'm not saying that all women who are not virgins are unfit to be in a relationship or get married, but a lot of women who have been seriously intimate with a lot of men tend to lose their feelings and emotions frame, and start judging men by their sex game, that's why today we have women on podcasts or talk shows who talk about comparison size of a man's private part, seriously, women today talk about wanting a man who has a "big dick size", I honestly don't think a woman who has never encountered a man will start saying something like this, unless her idiotic friends persuade her with that nonsense, and maybe you've seen something like this as well, there're those people who go around asking women what they like in a man, and a large percent of their answers is "someone with a big dick or a certain size", again this is why back then virginity was a top priority, if not a complete virgin then at least the lowest body count possible, but I guess our ancestors had more wisdom than us regrading this issue. And this is the answer as to why many men today are spending a lot of money on trying to buy enlargement pills or herbals, to increase their size and satisfy their women, and unbelievably, this business is booming. That's an idea for a business, if you want to get money, just sell some penis enlargement medications, or mix your own herbals for creating a strong sex drive, and before you know it, it'll expand, literally, I know some people who are making serious money by selling this, and most of their clients are the dick-driven men who want to be seen as champions in bed, you might say "well it's the only way to satisfy my woman, or it's the only way my girl can respect me, or it's what women today want anyways", and all this is true, so does that mean you'll be dependent on those medications or herbs your entire life just so your girl can respect you? You can answer that on your own though. So a damaged woman is one who's been with a lot of men to the extent that she can no longer decide properly what kind of a man is right for her, besides looking and comparing him to her previous ones, well in my opinion, some of these damaged women are the victims of broken promises from men who said they'll love them and later on marry them, but sadly, that promise went down the drain, a woman can't just damage herself, unless it's the ones who've been brainwashed by social media and peers into thinking that promiscuity, 304 and baddie lifestyle is the best thing ever, that's a whole different story, but some of these women who are now damaged, were the ones who loved a man and would give him anything, and the man promised to be with her and only her, yet something happened and it ended there, then came another and may have given the same promise, and it ended as the first one, then came another, and another, and from there on, the rest is history, her mind's been altered into changing men and having the urge to get satisfied, so really some of the women termed as damaged are just victims of men who played with their feelings and left them after getting what they want.

Which brings me to something else, we're seeing the rise of single mothers go up these days, the reason might be women who were married and decided to end the marriage on the reason of demanding child support and money from the man, but the other reason is that some of these women were impregnated by men who only needed to relieve themselves and were left alone to look after the children, the truth is that women can't get pregnant on their own, unless it's some kind of miracle, like I said before, men today are seriously, badly driven by lust and sexual urges to the point that they just want to relieve themselves anywhere, the results are sleeping with women who thought the man had good intentions yet something happened and she got pregnant, but the man after realizing that he's going to be an unplanned father, denies of everything, you see the bad thing about lust is that it only takes one minute to ruin your whole life, a whole day of feeling urges, yet just one minute of it can get you even mentally distressed, so after the man realizes the woman she slept with has gotten pregnant and he doesn't want that, it's now either the man rejects her and blocks her completely to seem as if nothing ever happened, or the man pressures the woman to get an abortion, but if the woman denies the abortion, then what's left is the woman to look after and take care of the child on her own, this is why it's very important to be careful with who you let yourself go to, a man may smooth talk you into believing that he's the one for you, when really his mind is just filled with a sex drive, a man filled with sex energy can literally do the impossible, if he doesn't talk to women, he will, why do you think there's a teaching of 'how to channel your sexual energy', because it's a very serious motivation or booster, but it just so happens that a man filled with it can tend to make or declare things that may leave even an innocent girl convinced that she's found the one for him, and even if she sleeps with him, he'll still be with her, turns out it might have just been his private part using his mouth to talk, back to the song "Thinking With My Dick", so typically it's not their brains that are thinking for them but rather their genitals, and the results are as we can see.

So from that explanation, we can see that now we have men who are dodging responsibilities, and it's true, a lot that is happening in the world today, apart from weird relationships and over-standard women, all this is the result of men unable to take responsibilities and do what men are supposed to do, instead they're focused on chasing women, competing to see who sleeps with more women, satisfying their sexual desires, no wonder we now have men termed as 'weak' or 'soy boys', because they don't want to accept responsibilities for what they've done and what's happening, a clear example is what we've just seen, men impregnating women just to satisfy their sexual urges, men becoming weak by copying what they see on TV just to impress a woman and be called Mr. Romantic, men looking for the shortest route possible to get a woman or achieve success to get a woman, men using and wasting resources and time just to get a girl to like them, sometimes I think maybe it's best for them to go through these heartbreaks on their own so they could learn a lesson, seriously, I understand the situation that most men today don't even know how to be masculine anymore, I mean seriously, they're taught to be like superheroes from movies by their relationship coaches, so rather than finding ways to actually become and understand what it means to be a man, the solution is to listen to online dating coaches on how to approach a girl, how to seduce, how to have sex and more weird stuff, look, there are a lot of books, or even podcasts that explain the masculinity of a man, apart from that you've got your father to teach you the ways of the manhood, yet you decide to waste your time listening to people who teach you how to approach women, let me ask you this, do you think if you were to actually focus on developing your masculinity frame, you would have trouble flirting or seducing or attracting women? The answer is NO, because being a man incorporates confidence, strength, decisive, purpose oriented and more, and this what attracts a woman, do you think during the ages of your grandfather or father there were dating coaches or experts? There weren't, so men maintained their masculine frame and yet still managed to bag a hot woman like your mother or grandmother, yet here you are watching how to videos on how to approach, seduce, flirt and talk to women, it's a shame honestly.

Speaking of masculine frame, there's a certain kind of assumption or habit that modern women have implanted into their minds in the dating game today, you may have heard from some of your dating coaches or even realized yourself that women are attracted to the bad boys, I've even heard some women claim that they seriously love bad boys, but what exactly is a bad boy? In a short explanation, it's simply a man who's confident, ambitious, self-disciplined, values respect and defies societal norms, so basically it's a man who stands on his masculinity frame apart from these weak men, soy boys, simps and feminine men, no wonder women are attracted to them. In a wider explanation, bad boys are men with a focused mentality, focused on themselves, focused on their goals, focused on their life, don't care what other people think about them, tend to find a way to survive on their own, aren't focused on chasing or trying to please women and more stuff like that, you can see bad boys are more determined on themselves rather than trying to keep up with the rat race of chasing sex and women, maybe it's because they know that women aren't a priority, and even if they wasted their time chasing and pleasing women it'll just mean using their resources to the point of becoming broke then left by their woman, so it's best to focus on their goals and life. But to me, it seems that women have it a bit confused here between a bad boy and a rebel. I mean it, just look at the distinction here, a so-called bad boy defies societal norms, displays confidence and self-assuredness, which are typically also shown by a rebel, so because of this, women get attached and attracted to the rebel, mistaking him for the bad boy, you may ask "so what's your point?, aren't they the same?", well in some aspects yes, they may possess familiar traits, but have you wondered why when women tend to go for the bad boy, later on they get dumped, used and played, not to point any fingers, but you, the man reading this may also have been a victim of getting dumped by your girlfriend and left for the bad boy under the reason that you were too nice or not adventurous enough, but after a while, maybe months or years, you run into the same girl who's now single, probably a single mother, already used up and played, and she starts remembering all the good you were to her, you may have wondered "what happened to her? I thought she wanted the bad boy", well first, there's karma, if you hurt someone don't expect your life will end up in a fairy tale, also, she just fell into the hands of a rebel, whom she confused as a bad boy, a rebel may have the traits of a bad boy, sure, but he doesn't exactly have the emotional connection required for a relationship, just hear me out, look at the rebels you see around you, hanging out in gangs, doing illegal stuff, sometimes getting into violence, some of them don't even have a thought of planning a future, does this seem like the right boyfriend, husband or father figure to you? However, most women just like the thrill of the man's arrogance, his confidence, his act of aggression, for some strange reason it turns them on, but sooner or later, she'll come to find out the hard way that he wasn't exactly the one for her. This is why most women at their prime years get into a lot of mess because of choosing the wrong partner, the rebel that they confuse with the bad boy, the bad boy sure may have familiar traits of confidence, ambitious, bravery, but what he doesn't have is the disrespectful attitude, harsh character and unkind habit, he's just really deep into his own life to make sure he's well planned for his future and the woman he's going to invite into his life.

This is why it's important for men to stay on their masculinity frame, brave, ambitious, focused, not driven by sex, not chasing after women, this is what a man stands on, or what he should stand on, instead, we now have men constantly searching "how to get and attract women, how to have harder sex with a woman, how to be the man that every woman wants", seriously, the internet is full of these searches, very few men are searching on "how to be a masculine man, how to grow as a man, what are the traits of a masculine man" or if not that at least they're searching "how to start a business, how to make money", at least this makes sense, men should be committed to bettering their lives not chasing after desires like sex and women, remember the saying "You'll lose a lot of money chasing after women, but you'll never lose women chasing after money", as a man remember what your priorities are, if you focus on your priorities and get labelled as a bad boy, that doesn't matter, as long as you know what you want, the men that are constantly chasing and seeking validation from women in my opinion are still just boys, they don't know what they want yet, if they did know then they wouldn't have their minds focused on those things. Here's a quick question though, "if woman has to choose between a simp or a woman pleaser and a rebel who's in prison, not a bad boy, a rebel, who do you think she'll choose over the other one?", that's easy, the rebel, despite him being in prison, arrogant or disrespectful, yet she'll still choose to go see him in prison everyday over hanging out with the weak man, because the rebel, despite he's attitude and characters, still inhibits masculine traits.

Another important note to the men is, the most important aspect of a man is responsibility, which a lot of men are dodging these days, it's a well-known fact that whatever happens in man's life, what he decides, what he does, what he chooses is completely his responsibility, yet today, modern men tend to avoid responsibilities, for instance; I explained that there's a lot of single mothers these days, and that women can't get pregnant on their own, the fact that most men today are driven by sex tends to make them get into a relationship with a woman for the reason of sex, and after that it's the 'I never knew you' attitude, but then what if that one or those multiple sex scenarios with the woman they were with turns into a pregnancy result, the result of driven by lust and desire literally gives birth to the women getting pregnant, and the news hits the man like a cinder block, well he didn't plan for that to happen, he just wanted the sex and off he goes, so what's next? Well that's easy, he just avoids the woman, because he only planned for the sex, he didn't plan on becoming a father, either she aborts it or he blocks her and act like nothing ever happened, "I'm not ready to be a father, I didn't plan for that, how do I know if that baby is even mine, I don't want to raise a child now" you didn't think of all this when you were getting ready to get intimate with that woman in bed, so the next best thing is to avoid and block her, it's actually a real shame on modern men. Apart from that, men who approach and date a girl despite her showing her red flags, yet he still chooses to ignore them and date her or even marry her and give her everything she wants, his friends warn him, his family tells him, his mind tries to reason that something's not right with this woman, she cheats on him, but yet he still chooses to listen to his heart and continue loving her, then when a certain heartbreaking scenario happens, he'll just complain that all women are scum, don't complain or blame the women, take responsibility for yourself as a man and accept that it was your own blinding heart that led you to do it, but sadly, the men we have today would rather blame someone else rather than accepting responsibilities for their actions and fixing them.

There's something in today's society called "pity relationship", in a simpler explanation, this is when a woman or even a man is approached or flirted over by the other gender, and instead of denying him or her because they don't reciprocate the same feeling, he or she decides to accept him or her out of pity and feeling sorry for them. Listen, one of the worst things you can experience in a relationship is being with someone who has accepted you, not because they love you too, but because they felt sorry for you and didn't want to hurt your feelings and they just pitied you, that's bad, because just know at any time you will get manipulated because you thought at first that person loves you too so it's only fair to do what they want or get them what they want, when in reality, they're just using you that's all. People like this secretly tend to have another partner behind the curtain that they are truly committing to, have you ever heard of stories where a man buys gifts for his woman, then later it turns out those gifts were given to another man, money, cars, expensive things like that, maybe you have or haven't, but stuff like that actually exists, because that man who's constantly giving was accepted by the woman out of pity, and now because he thought he was loved, he just keeps giving and giving without knowing he's feeding some other dude whom the woman is harboring, another reason as to why you should never accept love out of pity is it might bring disrespect, men picture this, you argue with a woman, then she says something like "be careful what you say, a lot of men more handsome, more richer and more good looking than you approached me, yet I still chose to be with you, there are far more better men than you but I decided to settle for you", upon hearing these words, you as a man, what exactly would you feel in your masculine frame? Probably shame, disrespected, unvalued, all because you got accepted out of pity, so if the question is "is it better to get directly rejected and heartbroken than to be accepted out of pity?", well, you tell me, which one do you think is better, get rejected and feel hurt, probably endure the pain of rejection for a couple of days then walk it off, or get accepted out of pity, later on get manipulated, used and disrespected and later on come to find out that the person you thought loved you never actually did and you wasted your time and resources just trying to please them while they were actually seeing someone else they claim to be better than you? I'll let you decide which one's better, but I guess some people won't understand it until they learn the hard way. And this actually works both ways, men get accepted by women out of pity, and even women sometimes get accepted by men out of pity, but they later find out that all along they were just used for sex or drained of their energy and resources, though, not to sound biased, but it's more common for men to get accepted out of pity, and this is actually pretty obvious, and I'm not stating this out biasness, but it's clearly seen nowadays as we watch our fellow men accepted yet get cheated on, disrespected and used just to satisfy a woman whom they thought had actual love for them, but surprisingly later she came to end up with another guy or married to someone else who was behind the curtains this whole time. Be very careful out there ladies and gentlemen, the world is wicked today.

Speaking of married, there's a certain habit that women today have, and by all means, it's just as wicked, women today prefer going out with married men, earlier on I said something about this, how young girls today are seen dating married men, and there are reasons for this. First of all, there's the perception that if a man has married and has a wife, then the man must have some value, if he's able to pull a woman and marry her and make her settle down, then the man must have something that is valuable that attracted that woman in the first place, this is a perception in young girls today, and because they see their fellow women settled down with that man, then they also want a piece of that man, for the married men let me ask you a question, after getting married, have you noticed that more girls suddenly get attracted to you for no reason? In the past, you may have gotten rejected a lot, but after marriage, suddenly they came running to you, even the most beautiful ones suddenly start flirting with you or just looking at you with admiration, for those who haven't observed this, you might want to properly check your surroundings, and I've heard a lot of these stories from married men, they claim that women start to notice them more, even some teenagers who aren't already married realize this concept , that after marriage, more women start flirting with them even more, if this has ever happened to you, or is still happening to you and you were wondering why it's like that, well now you have your answer, well, you have one of the answers. The other reason for this is that, again, we live in a modern world where men's masculinity is gradually declining, the rise of simps, femboys and nice guys, even women on social media nowadays are complaining that men are gone, and because of this, the logical solution in mind is to date or flirt with men that are already married, because they still have their masculinity seeing that they've even been able to settle down with a woman, so basically girls today are dating married old men because they believe that men, actual men are declining in number, but it's the truth, I can't blame them on this one because it's the modern men's fault, they wanted this. The situation of modern men is so bad, let me give you a brief of traits that the modern men have that's been summarized by men who know their masculinity frame;

* Strong and uncontrollable sexual urges and weird fetishes.
* Very low levels of testosterone and masculine strength.
* Lack emotional and intellectual intelligence.
* Constant jealousy.
* Expect quick success without consistency to work hard.
* They don't want the truth; they want to be pampered.
* Laziness.
* Complaining like a last born.
* Seek and thrive to gain constant and unnecessary validation and attention.

And if you take a look at it, that's the truth of the modern man today, a lot of grown-ups are complaining that the youth in this generation are really lazy and seriously engaging in constant sexual adventures, they mostly don't have a plan for the future, all they do is scroll through their phones and play video games indoor every day, they don't even know how to socialize, I mean it, you can find four or even five teens seated at one table, but everyone is busy with their phones, yet they still want to achieve quick success, all while being lazy. But in some hopes, at least there are some teens that managed to make ends meet and focused on the things that really matter and have earned their success at their mid-20s and are making seriously money, you'll find 23, 27 year olds on the internet making millions per week, whether they started a business early or they used the internet as their opportunity to make online money, but their struggle paid off, the same platforms that the lazy man today is using to seek constant gratification, are the same platforms that other youths are using to make millions and achieve their goals, so if they can do it, why can't you?

So you can see here that we've actually lost it in today's world, people are seeking gratification and pleasures and at the same time expecting to become successful in a quick amount of time, good luck with that. And because they've altered their minds to be allured by all this stuff, it's no wonder they've let social media do the thinking for them, that's why many people now are living the fake social media lifestyle, you can see a person posting cars, mansions, designer brands on Instagram, but as soon as you meet them face to face, you'll soon realize the meaning of the saying "Don't judge a book by its cover". These are the men we are expecting to become father figures of tomorrow and women we are expecting to become mothers of tomorrow; God help us all.

Apart from this, there's an issue of cheating, first, in today's modern relationships, who do you think cheats more, the men or women? In my opinion, women cheat more than men, but not to be biased, men also cheat on their women, but as compared to women, not that much, seriously, even to a point that there's a theory made up showcasing women having more than five partners may be enough proof to justify this, look, the honest truth is that women are more easily manipulated as compared to men, and by this I mean they're more easily deceived by their desires to the point that they want each man with a particular trait, a man who's handsome, a man who's rich, a man who's sexually appealing, a man who's attractive or jacked, that's why it's really frightening these days that one woman can be easily having 7 to 12 men, and regardless of age, whether it's a man in his 70s going out with a girl in her 20s or a guy in his 20s going out with a married women in her 50s, sure guys cheat too, but I don't think if a man can cheat on 10 different women at the same time, maybe you've heard or seen it, but in my defense I've honestly never seen it, and the sad part is that even the married women cheat outside with other men to the point where they get pregnant outside and convince the husband that it's their child when it honestly isn't, there are a lot of stories where men have been raising children that aren't theirs all because the woman cheated outside her marriage, and it's really devastating finding out all this time you've been raising someone else's kid and the woman hasn't even shown a sign of remorse, there's even a statement that suggests that "women cry after cheating not because they feel remorse and regret, but because they got caught", which means that those tears are only because she regrets getting caught and if she could have planned her steps better, then maybe she wouldn't have gotten caught, which also means that she could've continued cheating. But still, cheating works both ways for men and women, for a man it's a bit different, men cheat under circumstances like the woman she's with doesn't give him loyalty, respect or peace, in some circumstances they cheat under the craving of lust and desire like seeing a woman with a big butt or other lusty desires, but for women, they'll cheat if a guy makes her laugh more, if a guy makes her feel special, a guy that is attractive to other women, a guy who'll spend on her lavishly, a guy who pleases her in sex, a guy with a certain high status, and other ridiculous stuff. Now you do the comparison between these two, who often tend to cheat more between the guy and the girl? Honestly there are even confessions of some women actually saying that women cheat more than men, and this is also a reason as to why in relationships or marriages, a woman is not supposed to have male best friends, because that best friend may have something that's superior to the boyfriend which will in due time easily still the girl away. But all in all everybody cheats nowadays, it's a common thing, I'm not saying it's cool, but please ladies and gentlemen, have some class, you're hurting that person's heart, and fearfully remember the laws of karma, if you cheat on someone who loves you today to be with someone who you desire, sooner or later, that person you desire will also cheat on you for someone else better than you, leaving you also hurt and broken, what goes around, comes around.

There's a few things I want to make openly clear here, it has something to do with the modern women, first of all, there's the conception that women today are more afraid of diseases than they're afraid of pregnancy, and the other thing is that women today are looking for help not love. In today's world, one of the most heard words in a relationship is "abortion", it is seriously practiced a lot by women, some, like I explained earlier are victims to men who betrayed them and made them have abortions as they were not ready to become fathers, others had abortions intentionally, and by intentionally I'm speaking about the groups of slay queens, 304s, baddies and even OnlyFans girls, in my opinion these are the ones who are leading in enriching the abortion clinics, take it as an accident on the job kind of thing, after doing what they do for the money, attention or subscribers, if they found out that something didn't exactly go as planned and they got pregnant, not a problem, they've got pills on the go, and like I've said it before, these kind of women also have an influence on the youth women watching this, so it inspires them to do exactly what they see, if they see OnlyFans girls making a lot of money from it, they do it, if they see slay queens or 304s engaging in promiscuity to make money, they'll do it also, and in case something goes wrong on the job, and by something, I mean pregnancy, they'll just abort it and go on with their lives, so rather than worrying that what they're doing might have serious complications to their health or their mental state or even degrading their value, they choose to do it and just have P2 pills ready in their purses, that's why most men today have the perception that modern women today are more afraid of pregnancy than they're afraid of diseases.

And the other point that women today are looking for help and not love, in some aspects this might be true, it may apply to the single mothers, it may apply to just the regular teenagers, all in all there are women that are actually and sadly not interested in a man's love but in what he can offer her then off she goes, have you heard or witnessed some women who were funded their school or college fees by their boyfriends then after done with her studies, she dumped him, despite all he had done, or have you ever heard of a man, maybe a boyfriend or husband opened a business for his woman, then when the business started to take off, all of a sudden the woman started losing interest in the man, followed by the disrespect, then finally ended by the claim of divorce or being dumped, this is something that is sadly quite common now, this is why I'm reminding you, be careful with who you approach, people today are seriously doing a lot of pretending and acting, you can approach a woman and she may be all welcoming and sweet and kind, and tell you she's single, while she's actually married or has a boyfriend, but because she sees some potential in you that she might get, she'll pretend for you, and once she gets what she wanted, you're of no use to her anymore. I've heard and seen a lot of testimonies of men complaining that they did everything for a girl who thought had love for them, they paid her bills, funded her education fees, bought her needs, paid for her scholarships, opened a business for her and more, yet in the end they were dumped harshly or got married to some other random guy.

Look, nobody chooses to go through all this, but sometimes most people have to learn the hard way, some men know how to handle the dating game, and are the men that can get a girl without even spending a dime on her, and then there are those men who ignore their gut instincts, disregard red flags and every bad indicator from the girl and even if they get warned by their friends, they still neglect the advice and decide to follow their hearts, for these kind of men sometimes the best thing is to do is to let them find out the hard way through heart paining breakups, sometimes experiencing is believing.

On that point of breakups, it is a normally used concept today, a lot of breakups happening between boyfriend and girlfriend and husband and wife, and the crazy thing is that everybody seems to blame the other one for the breakup, have you ever seen a couple breakup and yet each one of them seems to be pointing the finger to the other person saying that he or she is the reason for the breakup, the woman will say it's the man's fault for the breakup, and the man will say it's the woman's fault for the breakup, which means unless you're a psychologist or a therapist, you won't know who's actually the reason for the breakup. Though, in my honest opinion, women are usually the ones who tend to blame the man for the breakup, maybe it's because women aren't very good at accepting their faults, even though it's their faults, but they won't accept the fact that they're the ones who've caused the breakup, whether it's because she cheated, betrayed the guy, lied or just drove the guy insane by not being a moral woman, maybe you've heard stories from women after a breakup, they'll always make it seem as if the guy is the one with the problems, they'll mark the guy as "he was too insecure, he cheated, he was always complaining, he was always noisy, always jealous to breaking point, demanding for weird things, never had time for her, and more stuff like that", sure, some of that may be true, but let's be honest here, a lot of times, most of those accusations are just false and it's just the women who refuse to accept the fact that they're the ones who caused the man to call it quits on the relationship. In a woman's story of breakup, as far as I've realized, a man is usually always depicted in three stages, the first stage is where the man seems to be the luckiest man in the world to get that woman, this is where the woman will say things like "a lot of men approached me, but I decided to settle for him, rich men offered to pay my expenses but I turned them down because I was with my guy, I get a lot of attention from many men but I always told my guy not to worry I'm only his", this scene will make the man she was with seem as if he was the one who found gold on a beach, the second stage is where the man is displayed as being the one with problems in the relationship, again the woman will play the victim card here, she'll say things like "the man was always jealous, he always wanted to keep track of me, where I went and what I did, he was always insecure, he was getting angry all the time and always shouting, he was never emotionally available for me, he never cared about my needs", this will make it seem as if the man was the reason for all the fights, quarrels, and arguments in the relationship, and finally the last stage, where after the breakup, the man will be shown to be seriously suffering because he lost the woman "after I broke up with him, he's grades started falling, I heard he couldn't eat or sleep, he lost a lot of weight and even got sick, he's embarrassed in front of his family because he promised them I will be his wife, he tried begging me to comeback but I refused", so here basically the man will be shown to be going through a lot of distress because he lost her. But there's sometimes a bonus stage, this is where the woman will explain that she was the reason for the man's success, his business thriving, his company growing, his investments expanding, all his success are because of the woman, when in reality she didn't even do anything. Again this may sometimes be true, but a lot of times it's just women not wanting to show themselves as the problem and blame the man instead, but in a man's case when you ask the reason for the breakup, let's be honest, most of times men don't want to talk about it, that's why some of them end up committing suicide, getting drunk, get sick, and if they do explain what happened it won't be a lot of story like from the woman's side, so you'll decide whose story is made up.

I said it before and I'll say it again, the dating market now is really messed up, some say the reason that women have high standards is because they're too educated, so what then, is it better to date or marry a woman who's illiterate? Well, some prefer it to be that way, the problem is that modern women are too accustomed to modernization and have crazy expectations, they believe they're entitled to some kind of treatment and special care, all while providing nothing important apart from sex, I already explained that sometimes just giving sex to a man is not enough, he doesn't need you to give him money or something like that, no, but sometimes he just needs your feminine traits, the care, the affection, a woman's duties to cook and clean while he's out there struggling to make ends meet, that's all it takes, but because modern women are too educated now, they think that stuff like that is of the past ages, they think that because women are now educated, they don't have to do stuff like that anymore, I've heard women say stuff like "how can women still cook and clean for their husbands today, a man has his own hands, let him do all those chores on his own", yet surprisingly, the women that say this kind of stuff are the ones that are either single mothers or even divorced more than three times, what's wrong, I thought you had it all figured out. But this is the hard truth, most women lose their sense of femininity just because they think they're now educated, they no longer have to be submissive or obedient to their men anymore, which just makes men lose more interest In women now, there're podcasts or interviews of women celebrities or public figures that are role models to some women who encourage and teach stuff like this, they influence most women that "roles between a man and a woman must be shared, a woman being submissive is a thing of the past, women no longer need to ask for permission from their man, women should also be the head of the family", and these teachings actually work, most women today get brainwashed into thinking that this is true and actually start practicing it, but for the women that want a successful happy marriage, before doing what these women figures are telling you to do, just take a quick background check on their relationship and marriage status, and you'll find out almost all of them are either single mothers or divorced, and ask yourself if you still want to do what they're telling you. Someone once said "It is better to marry an illiterate, submissive woman, than a rude, career woman who when you ask for a cup of tea after a tiresome day, she points at the microwave with her mouth. You will understand why a professor divorced his PhD wife and married the maid", and if you're not careful, you will actually find out. But in my opinion women who do manage to get a man and drive him like this, the man is either a weak man, a simp or has just lost his masculine frame, I don't think a man who knows his priority, standards and values will accept this kind of attitude from their woman, but if there are who tolerate this, I hope it works out well for you.

Last but not least, there's something I want to cover up on teachings that men are taught today on the basis of a relationship that is presumed to ensure the woman loves you, the topic that says "when in relationship with a woman, she must give you sex, if she doesn't, then she doesn't love you", you may have heard something like this or are also a student of this topic. Most dating coaches explain that in order to ensure that your woman loves you, ask her for sex and if she agrees, then she loves you, but if she doesn't, then she doesn't love you, that might be true, but there's one thing that you might be forgetting here, earlier on I said that sex today is one of the cheapest product you can buy, and if not buy, a woman can easily just use sex to get what she wants from a man, sure it's known that a woman will do anything for the man that she's drooling on, that's why you can use all your money to get her, but you'll hear she's easily getting undressed for somebody else for free, today most women use their private parts as a source of income, that's why I said be careful with who you approach, she may seem sweet and kind, but is seriously degraded on the inside, some men don't realize this, sure you may think she's your girlfriend and you spend all the time with her, spend on her and she gives you sex, but in the end once she's done with you, she's gone, what then, you've already had the sex and thought that she loves you, but then why did she left?

Sex today is just like business, like getting a massage, you pay and get your treatment, same with modern girls, you spend on her and she gives you sex to keep encouraging you to give more, but after she's gotten enough, it's bye-bye, that's why I recommend sex not to be the primary factor for a thriving relationship. So fine, you can listen to those teachings that her giving you sex is the indicator that she loves you, but remember, sometimes she may just be giving it to you because if she doesn't, you might stop giving her what she wants, and because she sees you as a man who can easily be manipulated by sex, she'll keep on using it to drain you while you keep giving and she keeps giving you sex, then when her plan is finally in motion, well, get ready to be amazed.

And finally I would like to ask just one question, "Who do you think should love the other more, should the man love the woman more than she loves him, or should the woman love the man more than he loves her?". There's a lot of debating on this question, some say the woman should love more, some say the man should love more, well which is it? In my opinion, the woman should love more than the man, not to be biased, but there's a reason for this, I explained that women are emotional beings, while men are intellectual beings, if you make a man love the woman more than she loves him, there's a very huge risk that the man will turn emotional and most likely end up being a simp or weak man, because instead of focusing on hustling and building and improving himself for his own benefit and his woman, he's mind is now going to be fixated on his woman, and eventually become obsessed, and one of the worst things a man can be is someone who is constantly obsessed with a woman, because he'll be using his time and energy to please her, his ability to say "no" to her or command her as a man will now escape from him, and in all honesty, if a woman sees that you've lost your manpower, then there's a big risk she'll start manipulating you or taking advantage of you or might even wonder what has happened to her man, the one who she thought was masculine, strong and resilient, but now he's all soft and pleasing all the time. Again, if you're a man doing this and all is working out for you, congratulations and good luck, but for most men who are weighing the scale on loving her more than she loves you, you really need to correct yourself before getting seriously hurt.

But if you take a look at it, when women love a man more than the man loves her, the man will be treated like a king, I promise you, this man will receive the special treatment most men dream of, this where I'm referring to the man getting sex from his woman without even asking for it, she'll cook, clean, care and look after his man, some women will say that's a form of slavery, but call it what you want, the woman loves her man and is thriving in her femininity while the man is thriving in his masculinity. Since women are emotional beings, if she loves the man more than he loves her, she'll be really committed to making sure her man is taken care of and happy being with her.

Though just an advice, remember, giving yourself to love someone is nice, just be sure the one you're giving your love to is reciprocating it in some way, if women can manipulate men on the basis that they love them more, then the cards can be played both ways, if she loves him more, then he too can take some advantage of it, so just remember to love where you also feel a sense of love. Men if you see your women love you, I mean really loves you, don't take advantage of that, if you don't feel the same, just be honest, it's better for someone to handle the pain of rejection than to handle the pain of being used, betrayed and played, don't start being mushy and soft, because you're a man, instead just be a man who can make her feel happy being in and showing her femininity, buy her a present, show her you appreciate her for doing what she's doing and handle her like your own woman, just remember to stay in your masculine lane.

The same for women, if you have deep love for a guy, just be sure he's showing you some response, love is a beautiful thing when you've got the one intended for you, but if you keep loving a man that's disrespecting you, cheats on you, abuses you, shows no gratitude or appreciation, then it might be time to let him go, sometimes it's better to stay alone for a while than to love someone who doesn't even give a smudge of the 'I love you too' vibe, some women have gone through that and now don't even want to believe that there are good men out there anymore, all because they glued themselves to men who weren't supposed to receive the love they got from those women.

So it all drains down to being with the right person for you, I can promise you, being in love with someone who's right for you is the best thing ever, you'll find out that love is sweet, but I can also promise you that being with the wrong person is one of the worst decisions you'll ever make and experience, you'll find out that love can also be bitter than a lemon. Don't ruin or waste a large part of your life falling in love with someone who's already clearly shown you that they're not worthy of you using your time on them, there are a lot of other better things to do in your life, hobbies, interests, things that make you happy, you know, some people end up finding their soulmates while doing the things they love, so don't force yourself to do it, otherwise you'll get one, but he won't exactly be the one intended for you.

MESSAGE TO THE MEN

To my fellow men, including the simps, nerds, femboys and the weak men. You seriously need to step up as a man, be accountable and be responsible for everything you do and say in your life, that also means in your relationship life, no one ever said life as a man is going to be easy, remember what I explained, in today's society, without you providing anything, you are seen as nothing, today, a man's value is measured according to his status, wealth, what he owns and runs, his physique, job description, talent, and more like that, but if you think this isn't true, then find your own way to adapt and survive in today's world and best of luck. But if you want to be taken seriously by society, your family and friends, even your wife or girlfriend, then you need to do what a man is supposed to do, build your masculine frame and hustle just like how your grandfather or father hustled before, there are so many men today getting lost in social media, getting tangled in what's known as thirst traps, this isn't a flex, getting hooked on internet porn and jerking off to a screen isn't a flex, going out with sugar mummies for their money isn't a flex, staying inside all day isn't a flex, watching and paying for OnlyFans isn't a flex, sleeping around with multiple women isn't a flex, none of those things is a flex to a man, there isn't a competition for being the most mushy and romantic guy, there isn't a competition for being the guy who has slept with the most women, but because your brain has been desensitized into thinking all this rubbish is now the new trend to the modern world, you think it's cool, when in reality it is not, a lot of men might not agree with me, but it's fine, the reason you might disagree is because you mostly let your phone and your penis do most of the thinking, that's why most men end up making stupid and irrational decisions in their life, driven by lust, playing with women then dumping them after you've gotten what you wanted, feeling lazy to hustle to get wealth, but you decide to find an easier and shorter route to success, that's why we have a lot of men turning homosexual, being sluggish, refusing to go outside, even men who are even afraid just to say "hi" to a woman, some are on the perception that they're a sigma male or a bad boy that's why they don't do stuff like that, my friend you are not, you're just an insecure, emotional driven, scared little man, if you were, you wouldn't need to prove to yourself that you're a sigma male, let society classify you according to your traits, but stop putting yourself in groups that you honestly don't belong in.

Listen, as a man, if you want to gain respect, in society or even your love affairs, then do the one thing that most men aren't doing today, whether intentionally or unintentionally, which is being a man, if you don't know what being a man is, then by all means go search the internet or even search for books, there are literally hundreds of books on the internet, even in bookshops or libraries that explain the nature and ways of a man, stop wasting your precious time scrolling through Instagram or TikTok or YouTube, unless you've found a way to make money through these channels, that's fine, but for those that are still studying, still looking for a job, still have no proper means of making money, weak health, body and immunity, this really isn't the time to be locking yourself indoors, going to every party, sleeping all the time, chasing women, getting drunk, fapping to imaginary girls you see on your screen, looking for rich sugar mummies to handle your finances, hustle, and I mean hustle. It's really saddening that the men in this generation are given the term "Weak men", because of what they're doing and what they've got their minds focused on, men today are focused on pleasing women just to get them to be their girlfriends, back then men used to go to war for their countries so they could live another day, but today men are fighting, using all their money and time to please a woman, and if it doesn't work out, he commits suicide, your grandfather didn't go through all that hard shit back then just to see you killing yourself or crying yourself to sleep just because a woman rejected or maybe embarrassed you, you got rejected, that's fine, she broke your heart, that's fine, she cheated on you, that's fine, get up, wipe off all your tears, go do something else, go to the gym, do what makes you happy while at the same time also makes you a man, you've ever heard of stories of men who got heart broken by a woman, but their comebacks got the woman who broke them regret ever doing it and start drooling on them? If you've ever heard or haven't heard, then believe me, these stories are real, not myths, but actual testimonies, these men knew that crying and sobbing all day won't get them anything, time is flying by, days pass and you are actually getting older, so there's no point in feeling sorry for yourself.

Do you see all these dating experts and coaches online, they might teach you to talk to women, how to approach girls, how to act, walk and talk in a cool manner, but I bet you a lot of them don't tell you the one most important thing you need to hear, that is "all that is easier when you maintain your masculine frame", our ancestors didn't have dating coaches or experts to teach them how to talk to women, they still bagged smoking hot women and married them, the secret is being the complete man comes with the full package, hit the gym and build yourself up, raise your testosterone, because seriously, the testosterone levels these days is really going down the chart, cultivate your mind, read books, stop listening to songs that get you feeling all emotional and make you feel like Prince Charming, life isn't a fairytale or a movie, life is the reality you are in now, and it is brutal for men who don't know what being a man actually is, some men today just complain "life is hard, women are difficult to approach, its hard finding a job", yeah that's true, so what's next? Just keep on complaining and hope one day you'll wake up and everything will be on reset and it'll be fine? Or get up and keep fighting? The choice is yours.

Something else important I want to encourage my fellow brothers, be careful, be very careful with the woman you choose to bring into your life, one of the worst things a man can decide or do in his life is choosing the wrong partner to spend his life with, there are important points to learn from your dating coaches, like spotting red flags or when to avoid her if she starts showing disrespect, these are important things to note. But if you ignore this kind of stuff and decide to do what your heart tells you to do, then you're diving headfirst onto a rock, if you think you can handle it, that's your choice, but for many men today who are seriously emotionally corrupt, need help on looking for important signals like these, otherwise, we'll be seeing a large number of men committing suicide just because they didn't understand the dating game in today's modern world.

My advice for you men, take it or leave it, stop pedestalizing women, stop treating women, especially today's modern women as if they're some kind of special beings or angels that are out of this world, if you get the right woman and you settle down with her, then treat her as your own special woman and make her feel that she's where she's supposed to be, but these modern women who are out here teaching themselves about promiscuity, being gold-diggers and slay queens, don't require your attention and energy, you're just wasting yourself trying to please them, and a lot of men out here is what they're doing, pedestalizing modern women, making them feel like gemstones, these are the same women who have slept with more than ten men and counting, will cheat on you with someone who maintains his masculinity frame, will disrespect you the first moment she senses your weak feminine traits like complaining, over jealousy, treating her like a princess, doing everything she wants, getting easily driven by sex and more stuff like that. So stop pedestalizing women, most women today just want attention, and as soon as they see you giving them exactly what they want, then just know they've got you hook, line and sinker. I feel really sad for the men today who complain that all the women today are bad, cunning, and have nothing to offer, not all of them my friend, you just happened to run into the ones who weren't right for you, and you actually saw all the signs indirectly or even directly telling you to abort the mission and back off, but you still chose to give her a chance and made yourself believe that people change and you thought you could change her.

Choose a woman that chooses you, stop choosing a woman that you completely see is trying to avoid you or is taking advantage of you, she's just depriving you of your resources and time, the soon you're sucked dry is the time you'll realize you've lost everything important in your life, whose fault do you think is that? It's yours, because you chose to be with a woman who wouldn't put you first in her life. There are some men who have the belief that religious women are the right ones, that's the first best approach at finding the right woman, but remember one thing, today, even the slay queens and gold-diggers go to church, sure women in the past were humble, religious and moral, but times have changed, even whores go to church today, so in my opinion, just seeing a girl going to church or being religiously active isn't the only trait to look at in getting the right woman for you, that's why it's crucial for you to take time to know a woman before taking it any further, she's got friends, look at the friends she's hanging around with, how she talks, how she behaves and acts like, what she does, how she treats people and even her past, things like these are important. There's one topic discussed in these modern times, "If a woman's past matters", does it really matter, the answer is "Yes, a woman's past matters", was she a hooker or a whore or a gold-digger, was she a cheater, did she have multiple partners in the past? Questions like these matter, don't tell yourself that it's the past and she has changed, you're not the one to change her, unless you're a pastor, but if not, then let God change her, some women even though did all that stuff in the past and finally ended up in your arms, unless they're changed by God, they'll still have those traits inside them, even though she had multiple partners, then stopped, be careful, it might not be your position to be with her as she may still have those characters inside her and later on do the same with you. Choose a woman that'll choose you, it's a real shame that men today choose women on the basis of their beauty, body shapes, curves, and make up, yet these are mostly the same men who later on complain that women today have nothing important to offer, well you wanted beauty and a big butt, so that's what she could offer you, be with a woman who'll make you feel like a king, respectable, caring, loving, nurturing, mother figure to your children, submissive, humble and loyal, a woman whom all of your colleagues will feel jealous seeing you get treated like a king in a mansion. This is the kind of woman you need in your life, but if you choose a woman on the basis of her being beautiful, her having a big butt and a chest, that's going to end up in a big disappointment for you, a Lamborghini may be good looking, sure, but it can't do the things a Toyota can do, so be wise in choosing. But some women actually come with the full package, if you manage to get one with all this and still have the desirable feminine traits, then you are one lucky man. And also remember, the kind of woman you choose will be your identity, especially in marriage, so if you choose the wrong one, your friends, family or even colleagues might get the wrong impression of you, even though you're not her habits, still, she's your woman which means you might have a messed up mind.

Stop chasing women, I'll say it again, stop chasing women, as a man, the least thing you need to do is chasing women, especially if you're a man who's still struggling to build your life up, women should be at the bottom your goals list. There are lots of men who've lost everything just by using most of their time on chasing women, this isn't a flex, nor is it a hobby, it shouldn't be your priority right now, why do you think women today are attracted to the men who have a masculine physique, are rich and are good at sex, these are the men who worked on themselves before inviting any woman into their lives, why do you think most successful male people, like artists, celebrities or even athletes give advice saying they focused on themselves first to become better and never wasted time on women, because they knew success will bring all the women they wanted, and that's what you should be doing, building yourself and improving to be better, now I'm not saying you should do all these just for women, primarily you should be doing this for your own sake and future, the rest will come on its own, but I guess attracting women may be one of the main reasons as to why most young men today are looking for easier shortcuts to get fame and money, that's why many young men today are getting raised by sugar mummies to get the money to attract women, becoming homosexual or even selling their souls to get fame and fortune, dousing themselves in enhancement pills just to get better in sex, all this in the name of getting women, modern men have lost the true purpose of being a man, and are doing all this nasty stuff just to get sex, I'm really ashamed of you modern men. You've probably heard a lot of times, maybe from motivational speakers or your mentors, a man needs three things to keep his focus on;

- ❖ Keep in shape; The first thing is to build your health up and your physique, build your immune and build your confidence.
- ❖ Make money; The obvious advice you heard a million times, build yourself up financially, men who don't struggle today to build up their financial status, are really having a difficult time out here and I think you can obviously see it.
- ❖ Keep you creative; Keep a constant flow of ideas in your mind, maybe ideas to make money, ideas to start a new business or investment, anything, as long as your mind isn't focused on searching for cheap sex.

Build/Improve your life, as a man, you don't need someone to repeat this statement for you, but focus on building yourself from the ground up, you see all those people you admire, those celebrities who have the nice cars, who have constant women, probably even your girlfriend drooling over them, they too started like you, they had nothing in their pockets or their lives, they were disrespected just like you, they were rejected by women just like you, at some point they even felt worthless just like you probably have too, but they kept on fighting day and night to get where they are now, and where you want to be, so improve yourself first, those women who disrespected you or rejected you today, will regret doing that after seeing what you've become when you actually decide to improve yourself first, be strong, be confidence, be a man of standards and principle, even if you finally get marked as a bad boy, even if you don't consider yourself as one, it doesn't matter, as long as you're on your masculine frame, remember, you're going to be some kid's father, so be a father who your son will look up to, a father who your kid will be proud to have and learn from, stop being weak and immature, be strong, resilient, a Godly man, respectable, a man who knows his duties, principles and standards, I honestly don't know the kind of children we will have in the coming years if the men we have today are weak, simps, emotional and feminine, that is if we do get to have children in the later years, I'm worried, but time will tell. And the fact that society today judges you on what you have, what you own or what you can do, shouldn't be the reason for you to hustle or build yourself, remember you're fighting for you and your family and future sake, don't fight for the sake of trying to impress, sure after your hustling, you can reward yourself with nice things, but just remember, the goal is to improve and preserve you and your future, and do it the right and legal way, even it means taking a long time, as a man, the characters you need to embrace is consistency and resilience, these characters will take you far, stop looking for easy routes or shortcuts, all those easy ways have a devastating price at the end that I honestly don't think you'll be able to pay up.

Stop playing or using women, one thing that men do today is play with women, there's a reason today men are regarded as just people who want sex and nothing else, just look at what men are doing today to women, make fake promises, impregnate them and ditch them, take advantage of the women who have honest love for them, that's not cool, and there's no award for sleeping around with the most women, you're just piling up more fatherless kids, single mothers and virginity-lost women, who told you that this is a flex? One of the most pathetic things I've ever heard is that men today have sex with a virgin woman who actually had love for him, then after the sex, tells her to just be friends with benefits, what kind of pathetic thing is that, that's somebody's sister and daughter, if you don't have any plans for them just leave them alone, if a woman approaches you and you honestly don't feel the same way, just tell her that you don't feel the same way, it's better for her to deal with the rejection than getting played and deprived of her dignity and left as a used scrap, sure women have their faults, but even some men today should honestly be ashamed of themselves. There's a confusing cycle going on around here, some or most men may want a woman who's a virgin, but finds a woman who's not a virgin and rejects her even though she convinces him that she loves him, because most men today are taught that women who aren't virgins are not good to date or marry because they might still hookup with their exes or other guys, unknowingly that the same woman was played by a guy that promised to be together with her forever, but after the sex, he went his own way, so honestly that's not cool, if you actually don't have any plans with that girl, just be direct, and stop densifying the society with single mothers, broken women and unmarried girls who are rejected because they lack some traits or possessions, some women out here honestly have loyalty and true love, but because they lack things like virginity, they get rejected, all because of some idiot guy's mind driven by lust to use a woman and depart from her, men, there has to be a line drawn for you as well, somethings are not a flex they're just plain stupid and immature, so realize that and fix yourself, most of the men that do this get their influence from the dating coaches or "experts" they see online, most of these coaches brag about going around and seducing a lot of women and getting to sleep with them on a day to day basis, and the men viewing this stuff decide to practice it in real life, though some tend to add their own methods, and eventually we get women who are played and used, that's why I advised that some of these teachings shouldn't be practiced, sure there is the sense of practicing just to build up your social skills, but just do it for the sake of being a man who's committed rather than for the pleasure of sleeping around and boasting that you've slept with a lot of women, that's not cool.

For the married men, stay on your lane. I explained earlier that in today's world, most women particularly the young women are more drawn to the married men, perhaps because that modern men are weak compared to older men, or because of the assumption of women thinking married men have something special or attractive that they've managed to get a woman to settle down, and now they want it too. That's why today, married men get flirted over and even seduced by young girls, are seen hanging around with young girls, and even some get caught by their wives sleeping around with young girls, some marriages today get broken just because the man was caught cheating with a younger woman, for the men doing all this, stop, you have a wife, you promised to commit to, you have children that respect and look up to you, how do you think they're going to feel catching you do all that junk? Some men even after getting flirted over by young women decide to take of their wedding ring and pose as if there's something wrong with his wife and marriage, if you're a man who does all this, shame on you, and second, if you weren't serious or ready to commit with your wife, then you shouldn't have married her in the first place, you could've just stayed single until you were ready to be serious and committed to get into a marriage, but embarrassingly you get caught hanging around and sleeping with a girl who might even be your daughter, some claim that they've lost the flavor or taste with their wives, well why not talk about it and fix it, rather than going to dangle on young girls, some men claim they were heavily seduced and couldn't resist the temptation, no, that just means you have no discipline over your sex life, nobody, and I mean nobody ever cheats by accident, you can't honestly expect me to believe that you planned somewhere to meet, got undressed and had sex and maybe even gave her money, and you say it was an accident, are you serious about your marriage life? Unless the young woman cast a spell on you, sure, that's a different story, but if not, then you my friend are not serious, I get that relationships are complicated, and stuff happens, but if something is not the same way for you, instead of cheating or humiliating yourself, why not just talk it out and work it out with your family, in case you don't know, most of the young women that flirt with you are also just after your money, they're giving you the title of "their sponsor" to support them financially, sadly, some men even later on tend to neglect their families and stop providing for them and continue sponsoring these young women, your wife and children are suffering while you're busy bribing young women out there, it's a real shame actually, some men claim that young women are tastier than their wives, in terms of intimacy, again that just means you have no control over your desires. Some men even claim that their wives have changed and no longer show them the best love as the younger women are showing them, first of all, if she's changed, how could you not recognize your wife's attitudes and character when you approached her back then, another reason to carefully get to know your partner before taking steps further, second, if she's changed, is the best solution really to start dating younger women? If the answer is yes for you, then you must be very proud, but I honestly don't think that's the solution to the problem, really you'll just be embarrassing and disrespecting yourself. So, for the married men, be careful and take it easy, a lot of married men are going through some serious traps falling into the hands of younger women, just learn to control yourself and remember, you chose the woman to marry and you have kids looking up to you, and you also have a respect to maintain as a man, don't throw all of that away on the embarrassing entrapment of getting caught cheating with a younger woman who's even young enough to be your daughter.

And what's even weirder is that, this issue is not only happening to the married men, but even just guys who have girlfriends, I mean it, today, guys who have a girlfriend get much more attention from other women compared to guys who are single, have you ever heard, seen or even might it ever happened to you that, when you get a girlfriend, her best friend also starts flirting or even hitting on you, for a reason you might not even know, the reason for this might still be because of the rapid decline of men in our society today, or the very same reason that women find a guy who already has a girl attractive, because he has a certain unique something that got him that girlfriend and now the other girls want it too, for some of you men, have you ever tried to compare the difference of what it's like when you were single and what it's like when you finally got a girlfriend, though it's not always like that, you may still get attention from women maybe because of your appearance, handsomeness, talent or whatever else, but in modern times it's like it's becoming more common for women to get attracted to men who already have a girlfriend. Sadly, and pathetically, I've even heard confessions of some modern women who say they don't want a single man, they want a man who already has a girlfriend, they'll have no problem at all in sharing, just because they assume that if a man is single then there must be something wrong with him to not get a girlfriend or to get rejected by women, either he's got nothing important to offer, or he's not rich, or he's bad at sex, or he's just not attractive enough, so the modern women tend to find a man who already has a girlfriend, just to see what's interesting about him. My fellow men, be careful, this is just a trap for you to get your relationships broken, if you accept it and think you can handle it, I can't stop you and it's your choice, but if you are serious about settling down and you're certain the woman with you is the perfect one, then avoid these modern day hookups and thirst traps, they've got nothing good for you rather than drain you and ruin your relationships.

Last but not least, as a man, respect matters, build your respect, respect others, and most of all, respect yourself, in what you do, what you say and what you decide, being a man means you have to struggle and fight to build your respect, especially today where a man's respect is based on what he has or what he can provide. Don't convey respect just on the outside to others, convey it even with your family, wife, kids, girlfriend, friends , everywhere a man should convey respect, even if you don't have what society expects of you yet, if you show that you're a man of respect who handles business, a man of his word, stands on his principles and standards, my friend you'll have the respect you deserve, even if it's in a relationship or marriage make sure you get respect from your woman, don't just take the reason of love to cover the multitude of disrespect you're getting, if a woman cheats on you, that's disrespect, if she disagrees and argues with you without rational meaning, that's a sign of disrespect, it's better for you to get respected than for her to tell you she loves you every day and disrespects you every day. You need to show that you're a man of respect, you've heard of the saying "Respect is earned", and that's true, but how do you expect to get it when you yourself don't portray that you're a man of respect, a man who knows when to be fun, yet be serious, a man who means what he says and does, a man who doesn't involve himself in embarrassing or degrading acts, to get respect, you have to show that you're a man worth respecting. As a man you are 100% responsible for your life, stop complaining that life isn't fair as if people will feel sorry for you, that's not the way of the man, being felt sorry for is for women and children, but as a man, whatever happens in your life is your responsibility, your burden, your cargo to carry and handle for the rest of your life.

Before I end this, one question that people keep in mind, "Should you forgive a woman who's cheated on you", in some teachings from online dating coaches, they say never forgive a woman who's cheated on you, ok, if you don't forgive then what should you do with her? Look, in my opinion as I said before, nobody ever cheats by accident, sure, and it might hurt finding out that the person you've loved and cared for so long ends up cheating with another guy, that hurts yes, but don't you think not forgiving is just going to be more of a burden to yourself, my advice is forgive for the sake of yourself and your heart, but because nobody ever cheats by accident, just let her go, unless you're the one that drove her into cheating , that's on you, but if not, just let it go and be grateful that you found out sooner before it got too late, forgive and let her go, for your sake, by not forgiving, you'll just be constantly thinking of her and finding a way to repay for what she's done, what's that all for? Forgive and let her go, some girls tend to start the crying attitude to please with you, remember, most women today, after seeing you taking her back despite what she's done, will make her disrespect you even more on the basis that you're not a man of principle or standards, so just forgive her, but let her go, it might not be the easy option, but it's the best option for you and your peace of mind. And what about on the marriage level, should you get a divorce or? Well some men do get a divorce after finding out, so if you think that it's the option that best suits you, it's up to you my brother, but, in some cases, if it reaches a point that your woman cheats on you, there could be a sign that you missed somewhere, it's either you ignored a red flag, or you're just not a man of principle to her, if a man shows seriousness in his standards that he is committed to having peace of mind and shows his woman that he is not a man to be played with, then I don't think it'll be easy for the woman to try something stupid like that, either way it's your choice.

So, to conclude my fellow men, remember, masculinity is the best thing for a man to get what he wants, do what a respectable, reasonable, committed man would do, for those who don't know the way and nature of a masculine man, I suggest you search and look it up, whether it's on the social media you waste time on, instead of searching for things that only fill and charge your sex desires and desensitize your brain. Be accountable, be respectable, be a man of your word, be consistent, be wise, don't rush into dating or marriage when you're clearly not ready, and always remember to maintain your reputation and status, because as a man in today's world, that's the most important thing for you, also realize that you're a man, even though modern women or society would term you as not a complete man for not having a job, a car, or whatever else, as you walk down the streets, you're still going to be recognizable as a man, nobody can ever change your gender, unless you do it yourself, but nobody will ever do that just because you don't own what everybody else expects you to have, so hustle because it's what a man was created to do and get your manhood discipline in order.

MESSAGE TO THE WOMEN

To my ladies, career women, young girls, feminine women and even the masculine women. The best thing you have as a woman is your femininity, that's the best thing you have and the best guarantee of you getting a good man and ending in a successful relationship and happy marriage, stop doing those silly stuff that online dating "experts" are telling you to do, unless they're teaching you to stay in your feminine lane, but if what they're telling you is to be promiscuous, manipulate men, how to use men, then you might want to reconsider who you're listening to. Look, in my opinion, the best relationship teacher and advisor for you to listen to, is your mother, just look at how your parents' marriage is going, if you see your parents' marriage still thriving, then observe and listen to what your mother is doing, is she being submissive to her husband? Is she cooking and cleaning for him? Is she being humble and obeying him? If it's what she's doing, then you've already gotten an answer to why their marriage is still standing, but if she's not, and you think what she's doing is still keeping the family and house together, then by all means, do what she's doing and see if it'll work out for you.

Stop having a feeling of entitlement, as a woman, stop showing that you're entitled to something from a man when you clearly aren't, a lot of you women today think that just because you're beautiful, you put on a ton of makeup, you have a big butt or a curvy shape, then you should get a man's money, wealth, live a luxury lifestyle paid by the man, all in exchange for your beauty and looks, while you don't cook for him, clean for him, don't give him any kind of emotional or even spiritual support, then my sister you're just lying to yourself, realize what a woman is actually supposed to do and to become to actually get a man who will do all those nice things for you, a woman who's obedient, humble, submissive, loyal and respectful doesn't even need to ask for anything, the man will give those things unconditionally if it's in his capability, it's not that he doesn't notice you being perfect for him, he does, so it'll be easy for him to give you all that stuff. And if you think that you're doing all that feminine stuff and he doesn't even seem to show the slightest appreciation or care and stills disrespects you, then you have every reason to leave him. And the issue of entitlement particularly goes to the women who regard themselves as beautiful, most beautiful women think that just because they're beautiful, then they should get everything they want from the man, that's not how it works, there are a lot of women out here who are exceptionally beautiful, yet single, unmarried or even single mothers, why? Because they had the same mentality that their beauty will give them all that they want and they set up a large number of unbelievable standards, standards of which not even 50% of them are achievable or possible, so they got ditched, played, used and left out, just look around, most of the women that do get married are actually the normal ones, the ones who may not be as beautiful as you, but showed submissiveness, humbleness and all that stuff, and don't think that men don't realize this, they do, that's why some, if not most men live by the code of "sleep around with the pretty girls, marry the regular ones", they know that beautiful girls have high expectations, high entitlement while offering nothing important, so you might want to check yourself and the standards you've well set for yourself in a man.

Stop promiscuity, this is not a flex, nor is it cool, nor is it a modern thing to do, this is just you degrading yourself, I explained earlier that a woman's value is like milk, it goes down way earlier than men, and especially with what you're doing in your youth years or your prime years, if you get drunk, sleep around, smoke or do drugs, display your private parts out in the media, just know there's a high chance your value will go down even before you hit your 30s, from there on no respectable man will want you, there are stories out there of women who were very close to getting married, but after the man found out about her past, all the drinking and the sleeping around and the cheating, he immediately called it off, you may think you've changed, that's the past, sure it may be the past and maybe you've convinced yourself that you've changed, but that's not a guarantee for the man to trust you that you won't revert back to what you enjoyed doing, that's why it's very essential for a woman to avoid promiscuity, I honestly don't know what pleasure you get in doing promiscuity, or what sensible reward you get from sleeping around with a bunch of men, but honestly you need to stop, what's the problem of just deciding that you don't want to play around with your body and value and wait for a proper man to come sweep you off your feet, I can't force you to stop and no one can honestly stop you too, but it's your body, your mind, your choice, would you rather sacrifice your happy ending for a successful relationship and marriage just for a few years of pleasure and fooling around or would you rather conceal yourself in your prime years, remain humble and obedient and get the right man for you sooner than expected?

A fact that modern women need to realize today is that, men are no longer obsessed with women anymore, that doesn't mean every man on earth doesn't want to engage with women anymore, but most men today are giving up on relationships and even giving up on marriage, because they're tired of what women are becoming these days, controlling, whores, manipulative, dominance, hardworking, arrogant, and the list goes on and on, some of you women may think that men are afraid of responsibilities, maybe there are that escape responsibilities, but a large number of them don't want to date or marry a woman who won't bring anything important in his life, and if you're a woman complaining that men today only want sex, maybe it's because it's the only thing you have to offer, maybe if women still stood in their feminine frame and didn't have higher levels of expectations and standards, things would've worked out.

For some strange reason, still unaware of, most women envy each other, women have jealousy for each other, whether hate for being more beautiful than them or seeing them in a thriving, happy relationship or marriage, that's why some women tend to be a source of conflicts in another woman's relationship, yes, some of you women whose relationships have been destroyed is because of your fellow women, women envy one another, and its well-known, if they see their fellow woman driving a nice car, has a good man in her life, is successful, they'll create some kind of hatred towards them, they won't show it directly of course, but it's there, and so they'll do what they can to ruin their fellow woman's happiness, a lot of women have lost their value by listening to their friends who had personal hate towards them, this particularly applies to the damaged women messing up the undamaged women, the women who've lost their value, their virginity, their status, their ability to attract a good man decide not to feel the misery themselves, so decide to share it with their fellow women, women honestly influence each other to do stupid things, get drunk, sleep around with men for money, manipulation, becoming slay queens and more degrading stuff like that, be careful who you call your friend and be careful who you let advise you, not everybody wants what's good for you. Let me tell you something, some men have figured out that one of the best way to recognize a woman who's worthy to date and marry is by looking at the kinds of friends she hangs out with, if your friends are clearly slay queens, 304s or gold-diggers, then I have some bad news for you my sister, it may be time to get some new friends before they ruin your life just because of their appearance, but if you're most likely by yourself or your friends are well known as moral, humble and obedient and even religious, then there may be a chance for you, so just be careful who you call friends, just their image could be an enough red flag to justify you.

Speaking of red flags, I suggest that it's also important for women to look at red and green flags in a man, the world is messed up today, even in the dating market and both for men and women, if you want to recognize a man who's perfect for you, for those who have good plans for a good marriage, I suggest you observe the obvious signs and decide whether he's right for you or not, some of you women have fallen into traps and have gotten played and used by men just because you ignored the signs indicating that there's something wrong with him, even if you love or loved him just ask yourself what's more important, self-happiness or living in bitterness with someone who's only taking you for granted? Sure, love is strong, but if something is taking your happiness away from you, you might want to reconsider, so in my opinion, red flags are important, read and understand the signs and decide if you still want to use your time on him, don't go with the notion that you've seen red flags in him but because you love him you can change him, don't do that please, you'll just be playing with hot coal, do what's best for you, and sometimes what's best is understanding a person and rejecting them regardless of the feelings you have.

For women who have established their own goals, like maintaining their virginity, NEVER let anyone talk you out of it, whether it's your best friends, your boyfriend who may clearly show you red flags, nobody, your virginity is one of the most, if not the most important aspect of your value as a woman, in today's world if you're a woman who has that goal and still a virgin, I sincerely congratulate you my sister, you are a diamond in a beach. In a world where a virgin woman is regarded as outdated or not modernized, show them that you know where your values are, don't listen to your female friends who keep trying to convince you to waste it, just because they've wasted theirs, that was their lost, not yours, even if they reject you, that's fine, in a few years you'll come to realize the reward of doing what you are doing, and furthermore, don't let your boyfriend talk you out of it, if you feel and have completely concluded that he's the one you're going to spend the rest of your life with in a happy marriage till the end, then the choice is yours, but if you notice him keep pushing and you've already discovered that something's not right with him, just deny it, even if he threatens to leave you, don't worry, remember, your goals are important and you'll get someone who's way better than him, a lot of women had the same goal, but because of pressure and threats from their boyfriends, they decided to give it up, and after that, the rest was history and are now regretting their actions, so if you're still a virgin and plan on saving it for marriage, maintain your goal, if your friends try to talk you out of it, they really just want to ruin your life, and that'll be just the first step in doing it, and if your boyfriend is pushing you to do it and you don't feel comfortable, he may honestly just be driven by his desires, but it's your choice so you decide what to do.

Another thing ladies, and some or even most of you may argue against this, but it's the truth, take it or leave it, stop setting up unbelievably high standards, sure its ok to have some standards you may want in a man, like saying you want a Christian man who's on fire for God, a man who's neat, smart, respectable, that's all ok, but what's not ok is saying you want a man that'll buy you an expensive car, a man who'll give you half or more of his salary, a man who'll always shower you with expensive gifts, a man who'll always spend on you even on unnecessary things, a man who's extremely handsome and good looking, a man who's famous, this is not ok, and that's why majority of men today are refusing to marry, because men don't want to keep up with these standards, you may say that it is a man's job to work hard and provide, sure that's true, but it's not written that he should work hard and buy for you an expensive car or do any of those things that you made up in your mind after being altered by social media, a lot of you women have made up these hard expectations because of what you see on social media, you see men buying expensive cars and houses and spoiling their girlfriends on Instagram with money and lavish lifestyles, but are you sure that's exactly what it's like on the other side of the screen? There are a lot of witnesses of men flaunting and spoiling women with expensive things on social media, yet turns out they were just scammers and got arrested, don't let the screen you're looking at fool you that all that stuff is achievable easily, there is an easy route for a man to achieve that but take it from me, you're not going to like it, but if all you want to see is the money, then fine it's up to you. If you keep having those weird and high standards and expectations, my sister you're going to get played like a football, some men have understood the dating game and know what you want and since they know it's hard to achieve all this, then the best way to catch your attention is to fake it and lie to you, a lot of you women out there have been played by men under the promise that he'll buy you a car, open a business for you, find you a good job, or him flashing a nice car or a big house, but in the end, after he slept with you suddenly he's gone cold, all that stuff he had were only rentals or not his, the promises he made for you were just air promises, he's disappeared, ghosted you, blocked you, acts like he doesn't know you, and you're here complaining that men only want sex, all men are dogs, men are liars, they did that because they knew it was the only way to get you to lay with them, maybe if you didn't have the expectations and standards that you have, then maybe that wouldn't have happened to you. But modern women's minds have been soo altered and brainwashed today into thinking that they can have everything they want from a man, and a man that can't provide any of that is nothing, many women decide to go for the already successful guys rather than the struggling guys because many of you women have the sense that you're entitled to be with a rich and wealthy guy while at the same time the hard truth is that you don't offer or provide anything important other than sex, just remember, if you think that just because you can use your sex to get him to give you everything you want, there are a lot of women who can give him sex too including prostitutes, so what's to differentiate between you and them, show a man that you're actually of some value, pray for him, support him, care for him, feed him, clean and cook for him, but if you think that's a thing of the past and all you want is money, then just sit back and keep hoping that your prince charming will fall out of the sky with a bag full of millions just to give you. Try to imagine one day men woke up and every one of them decided to set the standard that they want a woman who's a virgin and submissive and they're ready to spoil and spend a lot of money on those women, and they actually mean it, just be honest, how many of you women do you think will fit the post? But hey it would be their standards, you have yours and they have theirs, so be careful in what you wish for.

The concept of modern women wanting bad boys is leading a lot of women down the path of being termed as damaged women, earlier I explained that it's like women tend to confuse between a bad boy and a rebel, many of you ran to a guy thinking he was a bad boy and you may enjoy being with him, but it turns out you just ran into the arms of a rebel who used you for sex, cheated on you without regretting anything, played you, disrespected you and left you without a thought, the cost of you choosing a guy you thought was perfect just because of his arrogance behavior, be careful in choosing, I understand that in today's world the number of masculine men is constantly declining, but that doesn't mean all the men that are masculine are completely dried out, there are still plenty of responsible, mature, respectable men out there, you just have to choose wisely, you can't just look at a guy and see that he is arrogant and confident and be attracted to him saying you love his bad boy attitude, you better rethink your choice before they term you as a damaged woman too.

This is the problem of choosing a man based on weird preferences, as a respectable woman, you should be looking for a respectable man who's responsible, respects you, a father figure, moral, religious, smart, clean, and a hustler, stop looking for a man who drives an expensive car, has a mansion, not only has social media ruined you, but even movies or some series have damaged your brain into believing that the so called "bad boys" are better for you, just look at it, in the movies or series, the money, power, adventure, are all tied to a character who's portrayed as a bad boy, so that's where your mind has digested the concept that bad boys equals to good life, that's where you get it all wrong, those are just movies, that's not real life, in real life if you want a man who can spoil you, you have to show that you're of some value and that you're respectable for him to call you his woman, you get drunk, you sleep around with multiple men, you dress indecently, you demand for more without giving anything important, just how is a man supposed to take you seriously? That's why majority of women who once rejected a guy who wasn't a bad boy, later on come to regret it after seeing the bad boy she fell for was actually a rebel who just played you and now the guy you rejected has everything that you desired, but by then, it's too late, he's already found the perfect woman for him, the only thing you can do is just weep it all out, get those misconceptions out of your mind and start focusing on the real world and recognize your femininity, all in all, it's your own desires, but just remember, the life you live and the consequences that follow are the results of the choices that you made basing on your own desires.

For the women who are taking marriage for granted, please stop, marriage isn't a business, marriage isn't a one-way lane, marriage isn't a place for you as a woman to become the head of the family, another reason why men these days don't want to enter marriages, because modern women won't submit, because modern women treat it as a business to rack up the man's funding, because modern women show arrogance and want to be the leader of the family. Many of you women are listening to those so-called "role models", whether it's the musical artists, celebrities, or whoever, and the pathetic thing they teach is about being a boss lady who's independent and doesn't need a man nor does she need to be under a man, women are becoming so rebellious these days, we're being altered by social media and people who we see as role models, when they're actually destroying our lives, can't you think with your own mind what's best for you? You're letting someone else do the thinking for you, telling you to become like them and do what they're doing, there's the saying that "If you want to become successful, you have to learn from those who already have what you want", and I guess because you women view your fellow women on the TV or posting on social media flaunting the things that you also want, now decide to listen to her and do what she tells you to do expecting to have the same results, they're just messing up your lives, but I believe the best way for someone to find out the obvious truth that they're denying, is to let them try it out and they'll find it out for themselves, so go ahead and the live the social media and trending lifestyle and you'll soon find out the difference between reality and the screen life.

My final thought to you my sisters is, stop hypergamy, you're disrespecting and manipulating men who can't give you everything that you want and running to the ones who are already successful, if your mind has already been corrupted to make you think that you deserve a man who has everything, then go look for him, I'm saying this because I see a lot of women who are taking advantage of men who don't have everything but still trying to give the little they have while the women are still pursuing men who are rich, successful and wealthy, this isn't cool, just let the guy go, even if it means breaking his heart by rejection, some men are persistent, I understand, but just give it to him straight, he's a man he'll work through it, but some of you women decide not to miss the opportunity of getting some help for your desires and decide to manipulate and drain the poor guy, that's why in modern times, some women are called 'devils', because the things that you do like this, is actually wicked, you want a rich man, go look for him, you want a respectable man, make yourself respectable first, and please stop that silly notion of wanting men who are already married and already have girlfriends, I seriously don't know what goes on in women's heads sometimes, especially the modern women, how can you want a man who's already married or has a girlfriend, you think just because some guy doesn't have one or hasn't married yet, then there's something wrong with him, who told you that? You're just ruining another woman's happy marriage and relationship. If there's a married guy that's bringing himself to you, just reject him, he's just being controlled by his own stupid lust and desires and ruining his own marriage, but for most modern women, they decide to seize the opportunity and start going out with the married man or guy who has a girlfriend either for his money, status, fame or whatever else thing, you should really be ashamed of yourself for doing this, this isn't a flex, its stupidity on another level. Most modern women today find it easier to make themselves pretty by filling themselves with plastic bodies and turning themselves into bimbos just to attract the wealthy guy and neglect the hustling guy, well, there's a flow of statistics that I happened to run across while doing my research, preferably aiming at the women who think neglecting a certain guy because he doesn't fit the role for your claim of desires and want the successful guy, it goes like this;

- There are 7.8 billion people on planet earth, of which among those numbers;
  - ❖ 5.6 billion are women
  - ❖ 2.2 billion are men
- So, they advised women to be careful in showing attitudes to any man, because out of the 2.2 billion men;
  - ❖ 1 billion are already married
  - ❖ 130 million are in prison
  - ❖ 70 million are mentally ill
- That means we have about just 1 billion men available for marriage, and out of the 1 billion;
  - ❖ 50% are jobless
  - ❖ 3% are gay
  - ❖ 5% are catholic priests
  - ❖ 10% are your relatives
  - ❖ 35% are above 66 years
- So ladies, both married and singles, you have to rethink before treating any man like trash.

But hey I didn't make the statistics, they're a result of demographic report, and no matter what you may think, the hard truth still stays, women need to stop disrespecting men and start respecting them, even in a natural human factor, it's not cool to treat somebody with disrespect, you may claim to want respect but you yourself don't treat any man with respect, that's not how it works. And honestly there's a little game that a few men have started playing, men who are actually wealthy and have proper love, but instead of showing their wealth and status, they blend in and make themselves as regular guys in an attempt to find a woman who he can share pure love with, at first I have to admit, the results are actually disappointing as since most modern women actually want to see the flashy cars and expensive stuff in action, so they brutally and arrogantly reject and disrespect the guy who has what she wants without knowing it, you may think that he should have shown it, well, the question comes, if he did show you his riches, would you love him for him or for just his money? This is why I suggest, instead of trying to find a rich guy, why not make yourself worthy of getting the right rich guy, and I don't mean make yourself by getting tons of cosmetic and plastic surgeries, all those sexy stuff won't attract the respectable guy, it'll only attract the guy who wants to touch your body and nothing else, fix your attitude, recognize your feminine traits and embrace them that you're supposed to be submissive and humble and loyal, rather than trying equal yourself with a man demanding stuff that you honestly don't deserve, but if you honestly think that it's an outdated lifestyle, then by all means keep on listening to your role models and celebrities who keep teaching you about promiscuity, dominance, self-independence and more of that rubbish, the cold truth will hit you once you start realizing you're getting older, and look around to find that you're not married, single, a single mother, a sugar mummy, or just a woman who's constantly protesting for feminism, which will keep on pushing more men away, good luck.

So, to make a good conclusion, my sisters, please, try to recognize that you're important in this world, stop thinking of the stupid notion which is trending today whether men need women or whether women need men, its corrupting you to start thinking stupid thoughts in your mind and start urging you to protest that women don't need men, both men and women need each other, if we didn't then this world would've been only flooded by one gender, whether men completely or women completely, women are needed because you help populate the world and look and care after men, men are needed to build, protect and lead the world and also populate it, that's why we coexist under this sun, stop listening to somebody else who tells you anything different from that, maintain your femininity, no man likes a masculine woman, recognize your value, you deserve a good and proper man, if for some reason you thought you found one and he ended up cheating on you, which is something common today, then just let him go, because in all honesty, nobody cheats by accident, you deserve happiness and peace, but also, reconsider your standards and expectations, because if you keep on sticking to them, one thing is for sure, time will go by and none of your standards or expectations will be met, then from there on you'll start reducing those standards by yourself from a handsome, tall, spoiling, rich, well-built guy, all the way down to just a man who loves you genuinely, and from there on, there's a high probability you may end up like the other women complaining of why men don't approach them, this is where you'll start regretting your choices, start feeling sorry for yourself and some start piling up in the church crying to the pastors that they can't get married or get a good man, when the actual reason was your poor choices in a man have made you unapproachable. So take care of yourself, stay in your femininity lane, have respect and self-respect and maintain your morals as a woman, peace be with you.